A Stone for Benjamin

A Stone for Benjamin

FIONA GOLD KROLL

IGUANA

Copyright © 2013 Fiona Gold Kroll
Published by Iguana Books
720 Bathurst Street, Suite 303
Toronto, Ontario, Canada
M5V 2R4

All rights reserved. No part of this publication may be reproduced, stored in a retrieval system or transmitted, in any form or by any means, electronic, mechanical, recording or otherwise (except brief passages for purposes of review) without the prior permission of the author or a licence from The Canadian Copyright Licensing Agency (Access Copyright). For an Access Copyright licence, visit www.accesscopyright.ca or call toll free to 1-800-893-5777.

Publisher: Greg Ioannou
Editors: Marie-Lynn Hammond, Kate Unrau
Front cover design: Jane Awde Goodwin
Book layout design: Meghan Behse

Library and Archives Canada Cataloguing in Publication to come.

Kroll, Fiona Gold, 1948-, author
    A stone for Benjamin / Fiona Gold Kroll.

Issued also in electronic format.
ISBN 978-1-77180-007-5 (pbk.). — ISBN 978-1-77180-009-9 (Kindle). — ISBN 978-1-77180-008-2 (pdf). — ISBN 978-1-77180-010-5 (epub)

    1. Albaum, Benjamin, 1905-1943. 2. Soldiers — France — Biography.
3. Jews — France — Paris — Biography. 4. Auschwitz (Concentration camp) — Biography. 5. Holocaust, Jewish (1939-1945) — France. 6. World War,
1939-1945 — Deportations from France. I. Title.

DS135.F9A53 2013   940.53'18092   C2013-907067-2
                                                                                    C2013-907068-0

This is an original print edition of *A Stone for Benjamin*.

For Bob

In memory of Carole and Bernard, my parents

"... the most bestial, the most squalid and the most senseless of all their offences, namely, the mass deportation of Jews from France, with the pitiful horrors attendant upon the calculated and final scattering of families. This tragedy fills me with astonishment as well as with indignation, and it illustrates as nothing else can the utter degradation of the Nazi nature and theme, and degradation of all who lend themselves to its unnatural and perverted passions."

Winston S. Churchill – The House of Commons, September 1942

INTRODUCTION

My father is dying. He has slipped into a coma, and I hold his hand as he rests peacefully in his bed. He is in a private room in the hospice on the ground floor of a hospital near Toronto. Two Canada geese stand like sentries outside the window, and the sun shines brightly into the room with a promise of spring and life, exactly as he would have wanted it.

Orphaned by the age of ten, my father faced life with enthusiasm in spite of his loss. Whenever challenges presented themselves, he would get back up on his feet, choose to see the glass half full and move on. My parents remained married for almost sixty-five mostly-happy years, until my mother died ten months earlier. Following her death, my father's rapidly failing health came as no surprise.

I had an exceptional relationship with my father. If he refused to do something my mother wanted, she would say to me, "You speak to Dad. He'll listen to you." His love and encouragement remained unconditional throughout my life. When I began searching for my great-uncle Benjamin, who disappeared in 1941, my father became my biggest supporter and sounding board. Although Benjamin was my mother's uncle, my parents viewed both sides of the family as one. For my father, Benjamin was also his uncle — end of story.

Sitting beside my father a few days before he slipped into the coma, I held his frail hand in mine. His voice was weak as we discussed my search for Benjamin.

He turned his head towards me and said, "You have to write this book."

CHAPTER 1

I ran into her bedroom every morning, waiting patiently for Sheva to hand me a biscuit from the packet she kept tucked away in the night table beside her bed. We lived with my grandparents. My grandmother was a powerhouse, in personality if not in stature — she stood four feet, ten inches tall. I was too young to understand, and I didn't realize that Sheva was ill; she passed away when I was barely two years old. Despite my age at the time, I still remember some incidents that occurred back then, and my grandmother's face is etched in my memory. My grandfather's, too.

My mother and I visited my grandfather each week at his factory in the East End of London. Scooping me into his arms as soon as he saw me, my grandfather called me *mamela* ("little mother" in Yiddish). Sometimes I climbed on his lap while he brought his big, gentle hands around in front of me. He would carefully peel, core and slice an apple, and we would share it. Then he would take my small hand, covering it with his large, calloused fingers as we walked across the street together to Mr. Roumania's shop.

Standing on my toes, I would crane my neck in an effort to see the contents of the huge, clear glass jars of sweets lined up like soldiers on the shelves behind the counter. My grandfather waited patiently while I chose a mixture to take home with me. Mr. Roumania weighed the sweets and carefully poured them into a small, white paper bag. He held the two corners of the bag together then quickly tossed the bag over several times to create twists at each end ensuring the bag stayed closed. My grandfather paid him, but he accepted the money under protest — Mr. Roumania had known my grandfather since before the war.

My grandfather did not enjoy living alone and he remarried one year after Sheva died. He adored his grandchildren, and I loved watching him smile when I walked into a room. I always looked up to him; he made me feel safe. He died when I was eight. I wish I had known him longer.

My grandparents carried passports that identified them as Russian Poles, though they were Polish Jews who immigrated to London, England, where my parents, my brother and I were born. My family never discussed the Holocaust during my childhood, and the Hebrew school that I attended didn't teach the subject either. Though I knew that something terrible had happened to my grandparents' families during the war, I sensed that I was never to ask my mother about it. My father and I shared a common interest in history. An avid reader, my father had several books pertaining to World War II, though none of them were specifically about the Holocaust, a subject we never discussed in front of my mother.

My mother never read a book or saw a movie concerning the Holocaust, and whenever a documentary about the subject came on television, my father would quickly change the channel so as not to upset my mother. Privately I sought out documentaries and movies about the Holocaust and read as many books as I could find on the topic, though never at home.

The Jewish calendar contains many joyful celebrations, but as a young child I could never adjust to the sombre mood of Yom Kippur. The Day of Atonement, Yom Kippur is the time when Jews ask forgiveness for their sins of the previous year, and we remember all those people who are no longer with us.

The night before Yom Kippur, Jews light a remembrance candle at sunset in memory of the dead. The candle burns for at least twenty-four hours. We not only remember dead family members but also victims murdered during the Holocaust. All four of my grandparents were dead by the time I reached the age of eight, and my parents mourned the loss of their own parents along with the loss of several of their siblings. My mother usually ushered me out of the synagogue before prayers for those lost in the Holocaust began; I like to think that my parents tried to protect my childhood innocence for as long as possible. Fasting began at sunset the night before Yom Kippur. By the following morning, my mother always ended up with a full-blown migraine, but my parents went to synagogue and continued fasting for the entire day until one hour after the sunset. I couldn't understand why my mother would do something that made her so ill and so sad. I did not understand the significance of the day or of our prayers for the dead until I reached adulthood.

I was just a toddler at the time, but I remember the first time I saw my grandmother's family photo album. Most of the photographs of her family in Poland had discoloured, while others had a sepia hue to them, but I could see my ancestors' faces clearly. The musty black album was tied together with a tasseled gold cord, and I used to flip through the large book, trying to figure out my relationship to all the strange faces that peered back at me. I constantly asked my mother to tell me about the family, but when I asked what happened to them, she simply said they'd died. Relating the age of the photographs to the people pictured, I readily accepted her story.

I always returned to one photograph in particular: a picture taken in Paris of my grandmother's brother Benjamin with his wife and their baby daughter. Benjamin had his arm wrapped around his pretty young wife, who held their first-born child close to her face. Drawn to Benjamin, with his bright eyes, slight smile and thick, dark, curly hair, I intuited his strength of character and sense of self-worth.

My great-uncle Benjamin, his wife, Pessa, and baby Sara (with unidentified woman, seated). Paris, France, 1928.

Another photograph of the baby, taken shortly after her birth, shows her wearing an outfit that my mother remembered helping my grandmother choose from a store in London, and which Sheva sent to Benjamin and his family in Paris.

Sara, Benjamin's first born. Paris, 1928.

My mother often repeated to me the stories of life in Poland that my grandmother had told her. Even as a child, I could vividly imagine the small town where they'd lived and the family's daily activities. Between the stories I'd been told and that compelling photograph, Benjamin's life was already becoming real for me.

The stories always began the same way. Sheva, one of nine children born to Hasidic parents, Cylka and Szulima, lived on the outskirts of Radom in a small Polish town — though she tried, my mother could not remember its name. My great-grandfather Szulima spent his days studying at the yeshiva or synagogue, and my great-grandmother Cylka sold fruit and vegetables at the local market to help support the family. A poor, loving, tight-knit family who cared deeply for one another, they rarely complained about their lack of material possessions. As is the custom for Hasidim, my grandmother's family found her a match and she married at the age of nineteen, the first of her siblings to wed. Unimpressed the first time she met my grandfather, Sheva looked across the table with disappointment at her future husband, Moshe Aron, a skinny eighteen-year-old boy with a face full of pimples. Miracles do happen, though, even for a poor young student, and by the time my grandmother saw her fiancé again, just before their wedding, the pimples had all but disappeared. Standing under the *chuppah*, Sheva glanced at Moshe Aron through the thick veil that covered her face and saw a confident, handsome young man. My grandfather recited his commitment to my grandmother, promising to care for Sheva the rest of their lives. Then he broke a glass under his foot while all the guests shouted *mazel tov*!

Cylka and Szulima, my great-grandparents, with Dina, their youngest child. (Benjamin was the second youngest.)

My grandparents settled in the small village with my grandmother's family: a difficult transition for Moshe, who grew up in the bustling town of Lublin, about 120 kilometres away. My grandfather continued his rabbinical studies at the yeshiva, but he was a pragmatic man, and the reality of providing food and shelter for his young wife and his first child, Yankel, became increasingly difficult. My grandfather's two older sisters had already immigrated with their families to Glasgow, Scotland, and prior to World War II, Moshe decided to leave Poland in search of a better life in England.

Moshe Edelstein arrived in London conversant in Polish, Russian, Yiddish and Hebrew, but unable to speak English. Determined to quickly establish himself in England, Moshe apprenticed during the day as a sheet-metal worker and took English classes at night school. In spite of his full days of work and evenings spent studying a new language, he continued observing his Orthodox Jewish beliefs. Eventually, when working conditions became too harsh, he started his own business. He set up an orange crate on a street corner in London's East End, where many immigrant Jews lived. It is customary during Passover for observant Jews to turn over the kitchen, exchanging dishes and cookware with those reserved for use during the festival. Very few people could afford to buy separate pots and pans, so my grandfather re-tinned the interior of the pots, enabling his customers to use them during the holiday. My grandfather anglicized his first name and became known as Morris, and so began the establishment of M. Edelstein & Sons.

Morris spent the next two or three years working hard and saving as much money as possible. He also sent money to support Grandma Sheva and Yankel in Poland. Sheva put a little money aside each month and eventually saved enough to purchase train tickets and ships passage to England. My great-grandparents Szulima and Cylka wanted my grandmother to leave Yankel with them for fear of the *traifener medina*, the outside world. Sheva would not even consider leaving her son with her parents, and she left her village with Yankel in one hand and some loaves of bread tightly wrapped in cloth in the other, along with a bundle of clothing for the two of them.

They took the train southwest through Austria, where they stopped at the Jewish shelter in Vienna. Sheva turned her back while her famished son ate meat and gulped milk at the same time, breaking the strict dietary laws of Orthodox Jews, but she refused to remove food and nourishment from a starving child. My grandmother never again allowed her family to consume meat and dairy together. Somewhere along her journey to England, Sheva disposed of her *sheitel*, the wig that Orthodox women wear after they marry. In spite of Morris working instead of studying the Torah and Sheva not wearing a *sheitel*, my grandparents never compromised their religious traditions and continued to live as Orthodox Jews for the rest of their lives.

Sheva and Yankel spent the night in Vienna and continued on their journey to the port of Bremen, Germany. They crossed the rough North Sea by ship to England and landed in the welcoming arms of my grandfather Morris. My grandparents went on to have four more children, including my mother, all born in England.

Benjamin, Sheva's youngest brother, resolved early on to leave his homeland and make a life for himself. In Poland, Jews lived in abysmal conditions. Rampant anti-Semitism ranged from legal restrictions on trading with Jews to vicious pogroms, and the hatred was exacerbated by hunger, poverty and disease. In 1921, at the age of sixteen, Benjamin joined the exodus of Jews leaving Poland and made his way to Paris.

Benjamin, age sixteen. Radom, Poland, 1921. I find it fascinating to see the change from this conservative young man in Poland to the debonair man that Benjamin became in Paris, seven years later.

Around 1926, another of grandma Sheva's brothers, Yosef, stowed away on a Polish ship heading for England. During the journey, crew members discovered him hiding in the ship's cargo of potatoes, and British authorities held Yosef on board for one week before the ship returned to Poland. Government officials notified my grandmother and she visited him every day at the dangerous London dockyards. Sheva brought Yosef food since neither the ship's captain nor the dock authorities would provide him with nourishment. British authorities refused Yosef entry into England even though my grandparents promised to sign surety for him. The ship returned to Poland the following week where police arrested and imprisoned him on arrival. Eventually the courts freed Yosef and he returned to the family village near Radom.

Just prior to 1939, doors around the world closed quickly to Jewish immigrants. Szulima and Cylka died before the war, and Sheva tried to persuade those of her brothers and sisters still living in Poland and France to join her in England. As struggling immigrants, my grandparents had little in the way of savings, but they offered grandma Sheva's siblings financial assistance for their passage to Ireland. From there, my grandmother believed they could eventually obtain immigration papers to go to England. But Benjamin and my grandmother's sister Chava chose to remain in Paris, and the others all stayed in and around Radom. Having survived Polish and Russian pogroms in the past, they believed they could survive Nazi Germany.

During the 1930s, my grandparents and each of their working, adult children donated a portion of their weekly wages to a *tzedakah* box. It is customary for Jews to give a portion of their income to charity, and my grandmother's family in Poland desperately needed support. My grandparents could not afford to purchase a traditional *tzedakah* box, so they used a miniature copper English mailbox that belonged to my mother during her childhood. From time to time, grandma Sheva took money from the box to purchase sugar and other non-perishable foods for her family in Poland. Before mailing the parcels, she hid and secured items within the lining of much-needed clothing. My grandparents also sent money with family friends who continually travelled back and forth between England and Poland. This was the surest way to prevent money and food from being stolen during transit. My mother kept the copper money box for her entire life, and this treasured object now sits where I can see it every day.

Letters, photographs and postcards with greetings passed back and forth between London, Poland and Paris. The Nazis invaded Poland in September 1939, and by March 1941, letters from the family in Poland stopped arriving.

In the meantime, Benjamin served in the French army until the armistice in 1940. He headed back to Paris and began making plans to flee France for England with his family. My grandmother waited anxiously for news of their imminent arrival, but in May 1941 all communication from Benjamin stopped. After the war ended in 1945, grandma Sheva travelled weekly by bus to the Jewish Shelter in London's East End hoping for some news of her family, but as the weeks turned into months, and months turned into years, she gave up hope of ever finding any of them alive. The International Red Cross traced victims of the Holocaust, but information trickled in slowly, if at all, and deep down I believe my grandmother knew that the Nazis had murdered all of her family.

Eventually my grandfather told her that Nazi firing squads had murdered some family members living in the Radom ghetto and deported the others to the extermination camps of Treblinka or Majdanek. The fate of Benjamin and his family in France remained a mystery. Sheva struggled to accept the loss of her brothers and sisters, and her health quickly failed. She passed away in 1950 at the age of sixty-five. Grandma Sheva left my mother her Magen David (Star of David), which she had worn since childhood, her old wallet, her candlesticks and the black photo album with all her family photographs. I am now the keeper of all those treasured heirlooms, but Sheva's greatest legacies are the stories and photographs of her family in Poland and France that she passed down to her children and grandchildren.

My family immigrated to Canada in 1966 and my grandmother's photographs came with us. My mother removed them from the old black album for ease of transportation and then placed the photographs in a new album after we arrived in Canada. I married and had my own family but continued to be fascinated with my grandmother's family photographs. I frequently looked through them as I listened to my mother retell her mother's stories.

§

I began my search for Benjamin in 2004 with no more than his name, a photograph and the knowledge that he had lived in Paris prior to 1939.

Four years later and after trips to France and Poland, I had a filing cabinet overflowing with documents and research from which I managed to piece together his life and death. As his story unfolded, so did the personality of a man struggling to survive against insurmountable odds.

Benjamin stares out at me each day from the photo on my desk, and in spite of the fact that I am a realist, I occasionally sense his presence, as though he has stepped out of the photograph to stand beside me. I have never felt so close to someone whom I have never met.

CHAPTER 2

Gusting wind lashes rain against my office window. It is a Sunday afternoon late in November, and I have run out of excuses not to sort through the mountains of papers stacked precariously on my desk. With barely enough room to squeeze my laptop between the piles, I reluctantly begin the arduous task, filing or disposing of each page.

I see a file labelled "Mom and Dad's 50th Wedding Anniversary" at the bottom of one of the piles. I hosted the party for my parents almost twelve years ago, and I'm not sure how the folder ended up mixed in with my work papers. I open it and flip through the various invoices for the caterer and florist, guest lists and scraps of paper with handwritten notes in my usual illegible scribble. Mixed in with all the papers is a photocopy of my parents' *ketubah*, their Jewish marriage agreement, along with a copy of their British civil marriage licence. My parents married in Scotland during World War II on August 16, 1942. My Hebrew is rusty, and any attempt to read their *ketubah* proves futile, but I unfold and carefully read the long, narrow civil document. All the names of the signatories are familiar to me except that of my grandmother, whose maiden name is written as Albaum. And yet my mother had told the family that her name was Album. My curiosity has been aroused.

I call my mother and quiz her about the spelling.

"That was a clerical error," she immediately responds. "The registrar made a mistake." After all, she goes on to say, things were done hastily during the war.

"So you're sure that my grandmother's maiden name was Album, not Albaum," I say.

"Yes, yes, of course," she replies. My mother is blessed with a razor-sharp memory, even in her advanced years, and I decide not to push her any further.

My mother is the youngest and only surviving member of her family. She knows a great deal about my grandmother's family in Poland. But she is in her late seventies, and I realize that if I don't soon record the precious information in her head, it could be lost forever.

I call my mother back.

"Mom, can you put the kettle on and make a pot of tea?"

"Are you coming over?" she says.

"Yes," I tell her. "I think it's time for me to write down everything that you know about Grandma's family."

"Good idea, I'll warm through some scones, too." Mom loves to feed her family, even if we're not hungry.

The rain turns to sleet on my way over, and I'm cold from the dampness. As I sit on the comfortable sofa in the familiar warmth of my parents' living room, I look forward to hearing my mother repeat the same stories I've heard since I was a child. I cup both hands around the mug while I sip my hot tea, and Mom and Dad sit down across from me.

"Where do you want to begin?" she asks.

Pen poised, I say, "Let's start with all the names of Grandma's family: parents, brothers, sisters, cousins, anyone else you can think of, including those related by marriage, even if you're not one hundred percent sure."

She nods.

"Then I want to hear all the stories again, as Grandma told them to you."

As my mother speaks, I write down every detail and try to connect all of my relatives. It's a daunting task, because some of my cousins intermarried. Creating a family tree should be interesting, I chuckle to myself.

We talk about the many dynamics of my grandmother's family before the war: ninety-eight Albums in one town, constantly in and out of one another's houses.

"When was the last time Grandma heard from Benjamin?" I ask.

Mom looks thoughtful as she sips her tea. "Early in the war, I think he was trying to get papers for the family to escape to England, but suddenly his letters stopped coming."

Convinced that the Nazis murdered the entire family during the Holocaust, my mother tells me that she's nervous of "digging too deep" for fear of what we may discover. "I don't think I want to know the details," she says.

A Stone for Benjamin

"I understand what you're saying, Mom, but Benjamin disappeared without a trace, and we don't know what happened to him," I say. "We do know that he married and had at least one child. What if the child survived?"

My mother is quiet for a moment. "Yes, I suppose you're right," she finally says. "I'll help you in any way that I can, but I'll leave the digging and the letter writing to you."

My father, who has been listening mostly silently through all this, gets up to make more tea while Mom continues talking. It takes her almost an hour to retell the old stories. She gives me as much information as she can, including my grandmother's photographs. Some have handwritten messages in Yiddish and are addressed on the back to my grandmother from her sisters and brother Yosef in Poland, and there are two from Benjamin in Paris. Though my mother speaks Yiddish, she can't read or write it. I make a mental note to find someone who can translate the words on the back of Benjamin's Paris photographs for me.

I drive home carefully; the rain and sleet have turned into wet snow. Curiosity takes over and I cannot resist the urge to begin some research. I walk into my office, having almost forgotten what precipitated the afternoon's events, and my tidy desk takes me by surprise. I turn on my computer and stare at my home page, wondering where to begin. I have only a few names and some photographs. I know so little about the plight of the French Jews during World War II; I have no addresses for the family in Paris. All I know about the location of my grandmother's family in Poland is that they lived near Radom. I begin running searches on Google, and I bookmark, download and print every piece of information that seems relevant, translating the French documents as best I can.

The Central Database for Shoah Victims' Names at Yad Vashem in Jerusalem has recently gone online and I check out the website. I click on the database and run a search for Benjamin Album — last known address Paris — but the search is unsuccessful. I run a second search, changing the spelling to Albaum. I pull myself up in my chair, lean forward and hold my breath for a few seconds when two documents appear on the screen: one page of testimony from an individual and the other from a list of deportations from France. A slight shiver runs up my back when I open the two pages and carefully read each line.

The page of testimony states that Benjamin Albaum died in Auschwitz, Poland, at the age of thirty-eight; his parents' names were Szulima and Cylka, my great-grandparents. An acquaintance of Benjamin's, someone whose name I don't recognize, registered his death. I knew already that Benjamin had married, but at this point I am aware of only one child, and I do not know the name of his wife or daughter.

The other document is from a list of deportees sent to Auschwitz from Pithiviers, France; I run another search for any other Albaums living in Paris. A few names are listed, including Pessa, Sara, Frida and Roland Albaum, but I'm unsure of their connection to Benjamin. All four names are registered as deportees from France to Auschwitz. I print off copies of each document but continue to go back and forth between each page on my computer screen in disbelief. The results of my search at Yad Vashem are bittersweet. On the one hand, I can confirm the correct spelling of my grandmother's family name, and I now know the name of the village in Poland where they lived — Skaryszew; on the other hand, I now have confirmation of Benjamin's death. It is the wee hours of night, my eyes are puffy and tired, and I am sad. I climb into bed, toss and turn for what seems like hours and finally fall into a restless sleep.

I call my parents the following morning. My father answers the phone — to my relief. I don't want to explain to my mother why I need to speak with Dad.

"You're up early," he says in a cheerful voice. "Everything all right?"

"I'm fine," I say, "but I have something important to tell you. Are you sitting down?"

"Wow, this must be serious." I hear some muted shuffling and then he says, "Okay, I'm sitting down."

I take a deep breath. "I ran a search last night on the names database at Yad Vashem in Israel, and I have some news concerning Benjamin."

"Go on."

"Benjamin died in Auschwitz in 1943."

A long silence.

"Hello? Hello — Dad, are you still there?" I say urgently, wondering if we've been disconnected.

"Yes, I'm here," he says, his voice a little shaky. "I'm just ... a bit shocked. I'm relieved I'm sitting down."

"I felt the same way when I read the details last night," I say. On the positive side, I tell him, I now have the complete names of Mom's grandparents and the name of the town where they lived, and I am hopeful the information will help me in further searches.

"Do you think we should tell Mom?" I ask.

"No, not now," Dad says quickly. "The news will be a shock for her. We'll find an appropriate time."

I thank him for his support and tell him I'm not sure I could do all this digging without it.

"I'll always be here for you. Always," he replies. I tell him I love him.

"I love you, too," he says.

The photograph of Benjamin that I have looked at since childhood is beginning to come alive. I am determined to uncover as much information as I can about him and his family; Google becomes my best friend. I send out numerous letters by email and regular mail to institutions in France, Poland and Germany, including the International Red Cross; the Mémorial de la Shoah in Paris; the archives in Radom, Lublin, Auschwitz and Majdanek; the French military archives; and the Paris police archives. I do not speak Polish and my French is limited, but somehow I make myself understood with the help of a translator and friends who translate my letters and the responses that arrive from Poland. I leave no door unopened.

The Mémorial de la Shoah provides me with copies of some of the documents pertaining to Benjamin's arrest as well as copies of convoy lists. Benjamin's arrest card contains his last known address in Paris along with the names of his children, Sara, Frida and Roland: the same names I found that first night in the Yad Vashem database. I am finally able to piece the family together though I am unable to confirm that Pessa Albaum is Benjamin's wife until I uncover the convoy list that includes Sara: they are listed as both having the same address in Paris.

§

I now know something of Benjamin's death. From the stories handed down from my grandmother and mother, I already know a little of his life.

After my great-uncle Benjamin's birth in 1905, his seven older sisters, including my grandmother Sheva, adored and spoiled him. Benjamin was the youngest of two sons and second youngest of the nine children born to Cylka and Szulima Albaum in Skaryszew — the town whose name I now know. He attended a small yeshiva, developed an extensive knowledge of the Talmud and became proficient in reading and writing Hebrew. He also spoke Yiddish and a little Polish.

Cylka and Szulima with five of their daughters and their eldest son, Yosef, and his fiancée (though they later broke off the engagement). Missing from the picture is my grandmother, Sheva, who had already left for England, and Miriam, absent for unknown reasons. The little boy is possibly her son. Missing also is Benjamin, so I assume the photo was taken after 1921.

Not unlike many Hasidic parents, Cylka and Szulima had high hopes that their son would eventually become a rabbi. But while Orthodox Jews lived an insular life, the younger generation, including Benjamin, became increasingly aware of the changing world at large. Inquisitive and strong-willed, he clashed with his teachers on many occasions but succeeded in all areas of his studies, Sheva recalled.

At thirteen, after his bar mitzvah, Benjamin travelled the fourteen-kilometre road each day to Radom, where he attended a larger yeshiva. Radom had a substantial Jewish community with several Jewish political organizations and clubs as well as Jewish businesses, including kosher butchers, fish shops, photography studios, taverns, and bookstores selling Hebrew and Yiddish newspapers. Benjamin occasionally met his friends at cafés in Radom and frequently overheard lively political discussion and debate. Life for Polish Jews became increasingly difficult, with anti-Semitism growing and pogroms occurring regularly. Disease, hunger and poverty became commonplace, exacerbated by restrictions on trading with Jews and making life insufferable in countless villages and towns, including Skaryszew.

In 1921, Benjamin turned sixteen and plucked up the courage to tell his parents that he would not become a rabbi. He also decided he could no longer live in Poland. Determined to join the exodus of Jews leaving Poland, Benjamin worked at odd jobs until he saved sufficient money to pay for his train ticket out of the country. A married elder sister lived in Paris, and he convinced his parents he would be fine there. (One of his sisters lived in England, but he chose Paris, and I like to think this reveals something about his personality and inclinations.)

Unable to change Benjamin's rebellious mind, Cylka and Szulima kissed and hugged their youngest son goodbye at the train station; little did any of them know that they would never see one another again.

§

Benjamin arrived in Paris in December 1921 at the start of the Roaring Twenties. Now that World War I was over, the French were ready to embrace life with exuberance. It was easy to find jobs in the growing economy, and people spent money freely, dining in cafes and restaurants and going to the theatre. Writers such as Gertrude Stein, F. Scott Fitzgerald and Ernest Hemingway were living in Paris, and the American jazz singer Josephine Baker turned the heads of Parisians with her provocative stage shows. Art deco style influenced everything in the creative arts. Women felt emancipated when it came to fashion. Coco Chanel, already a popular designer, introduced beautiful new styles of clothing for women, and her famous pearl necklace became the accessory of choice. I wish I could have seen Benjamin's face while he took in the sights of Paris for the first time.

Benjamin's arrival in Paris could not have been more opportune for a young man, and I suspect he embraced the city's joie de vivre during those années folles while he matured from boy to man. A thriving Jewish community in Paris made it easy for him to find a job working in a factory making handmade ladies' leather gloves.

Benjamin spoke Yiddish but learned to speak fluent French. He styled his wavy black hair in a sort of pompadour and wore fashionable clothing. I wonder if he learned to dance or met his friends at bistros and cafés in the Marais. I think he must have revelled in his new life in Paris, which was certainly a far cry from the Hasidic culture that he'd left behind in Skaryszew. In 1927 Benjamin, at twenty-two, met Pessa, a fourteen-year-old Jewish immigrant from Warsaw. With her slender figure, large dark eyes and hair neatly cropped into a stylish bob — clearly not an Orthodox Jew — Pessa appeared older than her years. The young couple fell in love, and though Pessa was slightly taller than Benjamin, they made a handsome couple. I like to picture them embracing the 1920s in Paris, joining friends at jazz clubs and dancing late into the evening.

Pessa turned fifteen in January 1928 and married Benjamin within a few days of his birthday the same month. They lived in Saint-Ouen, a suburb of Paris just north of the Marais district. Benjamin soon set up shop as a *brocanteur*, a dealer of second-hand goods and antiques.

As an adult, I look again at the photograph that captivated me so much as a child. I know now that it was taken in celebration of the Jewish New Year. Benjamin's eyes stare back at me with strength and determination, while beside him, Pessa is chic in a sleeveless flapper dress and Chanel-style beads. She holds their first-born child, Sara, in her arms, and a baby bottle full of milk sits on a table beside them, perhaps to soothe the baby between poses.[1] I also know now that Pessa and Benjamin had two more children: another daughter, Frida, born in 1931, and a son, Roland, born in 1933.

On the back of the photo, in Hebrew, Benjamin has written, "To my dear sister Sheva. I am sending this picture as an indication of life and of your brother Benjamin, 12 September 1928." "Life," no doubt, refers to the baby, Sara. In the photo, Benjamin, his arm about Pessa's waist, looks happy and proud of his family.

---

1. As an adult, I'd assumed the seated woman in the photo was Benjamin's mother-in-law, but my mother told me the woman was unrelated to the family. She said it was not unusual for people to join together in one photo shoot for the High Holidays rather than pay for two separate sittings.

CHAPTER 3

Benjamin's comfortable life with his young family came crashing to a halt after World War II began on September 1, 1939, when Nazi Germany invaded Poland. France allied with Great Britain and declared war on Germany. Benjamin joined the army and fought against Germany with his fellow Frenchmen. But war did not last long for the French. On June 22, 1940, France surrendered to Germany and the Nazis occupied northern France, including Paris.

After France signed an armistice with Germany, the French army relieved thousands of soldiers of their duties including Benjamin, who returned to his family in Paris.

Then the French government implemented the *statuts des juifs*, laws that discriminated against French Jews. This was quickly followed by a decree authorizing the arrest and detention of Jews born outside of France and a bill barring Jews from working in government or in schools.

Benjamin and his family lived at 6 villa Condorcet on the edge of the Marais, an area of Paris highly populated by immigrant Jews. By 1939 he had lived in France for eighteen years.

By September 1940, all Jews were required to be registered with the French authorities. French Jews suffered greatly under continued government restrictions. A shortened list of permitted work was issued toward the end of the year and it directly affected Benjamin. The list excluded the trading of antiques, and as a *brocanteur*, Benjamin lost his livelihood.

In 1941 all Jews were required to wear a yellow star with the word *Juif* (Jew) in the centre. Benjamin was one of several thousand Jewish men who received a demand to report to a police station located in Paris on May 14, 1941, for questioning.

Most of the men who reported for questioning believed they would not be detained since they lived and worked in France legally. Benjamin presented himself at the police station, probably confident that as soon as police verified his identity, he would be registered and sent on his way. But that did not happen, and when he was further interrogated by the French police, he must have been gripped with fear for his life, and for the lives of his family.

```
NOM : ALBAUM
PRÉNOMS : Benjamin
Date et lieu de naissance : 15-I-1905 à Radom
                                        N° du Dossier juif : 64307
SEXE : masculin
NATIONALITÉ : polonaise
PROFESSION : brocanteur commerçant
ADRESSE : 6, Villa Condorcet
          SAINT-OUEN

SITUATION de famille : marié
CONJOINT : juive

                Prénoms    | Date et lieu de naissance | Nationalité
ENFANTS         Sara       | 1928                      | frse
de moins        Frida      | 1931                      |  "
de 15 ans       Roland     | 1933                      |  "
et à charge

INFIRMITÉS :

SERVICES de GUERRE : 39-40 armée frse
   2ème classe

SITUATION
administrative
de l'étranger

N° du casier central : 548522
REMARQUES PARTICULIÈRES :

                RECHERCHÉ
                265-E — Imp. Chaix (R). — 1591-41
```

Benjamin's arrest record. (Courtesy of Mémorial de la Shoah.)

During his questioning, police asked Benjamin to identify his mother by name and nationality, thus proving his ethnicity, *juif*. According to registration documents, when asked about his family, Benjamin identified only his children by name and age; perhaps he felt confident that the children, all born in France, faced no danger of being arrested.

Benjamin did not identify Pessa by name, no doubt in an attempt to shield his wife, who had not been born in France. But police recorded her religion as juive — and now they had her address.

Little did Benjamin know that the names and addresses of next of kin gave the police easy access to their next victims. When the police confiscated all his identity cards, he must have felt a deep dread. It did not take long for them to issue him a second card, a document that sealed his fate.

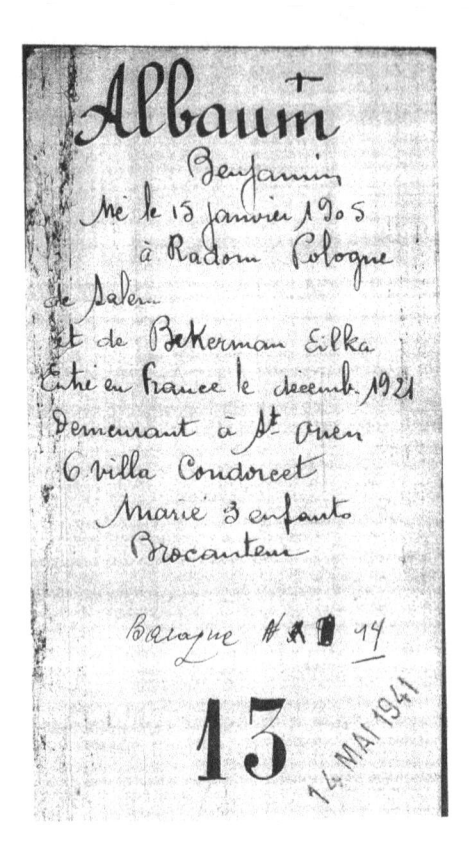

Interrogation document showing Benjamin's mother's maiden name, Bekerman. (Courtesy of Mémorial de la Shoah.)

After police completed their interrogation, Benjamin was transported by bus to Gare d'Austerlitz train station, where he boarded a waiting train that departed for the French concentration camp of Pithiviers, approximately eighty kilometers south of Paris.

While all this was going on, Benjamin had no way of contacting Pessa. I cannot imagine what must have been going through her head as she anxiously waited for Benjamin to come home. One month later, in June 1941, authorities finally notified Pessa of Benjamin's arrest and internment in Pithiviers.

Living conditions in the camp were terrible. Initially, visiting was not allowed, however police eventually permitted wives and relatives to see their husbands and family members. Eventually French police allowed the men to work for each other doing various odd jobs. Benjamin worked at local farms as an agricultural worker, but agricultural workers made very little money, so it is unlikely that he was able to help support Pessa and the children.

Even before Benjamin's arrest, the family must have struggled to make ends meet since he could no longer operate his business. Benjamin and Pessa possibly took odd jobs to earn some income. But after Benjamin's arrest and internment in Pithiviers, supporting the family fell squarely on Pessa's shoulders. Most families received food stamps, and some had assistance from various Jewish agencies operating in France. These groups were primarily funded by financial donations from Jews around the world, but as the war went on, they would have been increasingly constrained. Pessa must have felt fear and hopelessness while she cared for her three children alone; as days turned into months, the future looked increasingly bleak.

I am sure Pessa would have visited Benjamin at Pithiviers at least once during the fourteen months he remained there. While I have no proof, at least this thought gives me some small scrap of comfort.

§

The first convoy from France to Auschwitz left on March 27, 1942. It was possibly the only train to leave France in which prisoners travelled in third-class carriages. Approximately 1200 prisoners were on board. The French national railway, the Société nationale des chemins de fer (SNCF) began deportations using their engines and engineers. Although the SNCF subsequently supplied cattle cars, they continued to charge the Nazis third-class carriage fares for all convoys to Auschwitz. The average convoy transported 1000 victims to the camp.

Unbeknownst to Benjamin, French police arrested Pessa and their three children on July 16, 1942, the day before his departure for Auschwitz. Early in the morning of July 17, after fourteen months of imprisonment in appalling conditions, Benjamin Albaum's dreaded deportation began.

The Nazis, in consultation with French camp commanders, were reducing the population of Pithiviers in preparation for the arrival of thousands of Jews recently detained in Paris after a mass arrest. There were 928 prisoners, including the acclaimed French author Irene Nemirovsky, packed into tightly-sealed cattle cars in the sweltering summer heat without food or water. Prisoners endured the journey in discomfort and trepidation. Convoy 6 left Pithiviers at 6:15 a.m. and took two days to reach Auschwitz.

Below is my English translation of the official transcript from the Mémorial de la Shoah about this convoy:

CONVOY 6, July 17, 1942:

The convoy left the camp of Pithiviers, with 809 men and 119 women; a total of 928 people were deported. A telex was sent on July 18 from the commander of SiPo-SD [the Nazi police force] in Orleans along with the anti-Jewish section (IVJ) of the Gestapo in Paris, confirming the exact number of deportees, which included 193 male and female Jews who were sent by the commando of SiPo in Dijon along with 52 others who came from the commando of Orleans. The telex adds that two original lists were given to the chief of the convoy, Lieutenant Schneider of the French police.

The list of names was a copy and almost illegible since mauve carbon paper was used. The list of deportees specified the last names, first names, dates and birthplaces, professions and cities of residence. The spelling of some of the names may have been incorrect.

Most of the deportees came from the Paris area. Nationality was not specified on the list, but by looking at the birthplaces of the deportees, the majority were originally from Poland.

The age bracket ranged between 33 and 42 years (550 out of 928 deportees). There were 141 teenagers between 16 and 22 years who were accompanied by their parents. There were also even younger children, including 12 year old Marie-Louise Warenbron, born in Paris, April 27, 1930, and 13 year old Rebecca Nowodzorski, born in Luxembourg, September 13, 1928.

There were two documents from the Gestapo pertaining to this convoy: (XXVb-75) of July 14 and a telex of July 17 from the anti-Jewish section of the Gestapo in Paris sent to Eichmann in Berlin [and to] the camp of Sachsenhausen in Oranienburg and the commander of Auschwitz. The telex stated that the convoy left Pithiviers, July 17 at 6h 15.

On arrival in Auschwitz on July 19, 809 men received [tattoo] numbers 48880 to 49688 and 119 women received numbers 9550 to 9668.

In 1945, there were 18 survivors of the convoy.

I now know the date of Benjamin's deportation and the date and place of his death, ten months later. It remains to be seen if I will ever find out anything about what he lived through during that time.

§

On July 16, 1942, a mass roundup of Jews, commonly known as the Vel d'Hiv raid, began in the early hours of the morning. Pessa Albaum and her children Sara, Roland and Frida were taken into custody and escorted onto buses with other families and then driven to the Vélodrome d'Hiver, an indoor sports stadium in Paris. More than 12,000 Jews were arrested that day and held in the stadium for several days in inexcusable conditions. The stifling summer heat made the interior of the stadium unbearable. With barely any water or food and a repulsive stench emanating from insufficient and overflowing toilets, sleep became impossible. Numerous suicides occurred, and given the layout of the stadium, it would have been difficult for Pessa to shield the children's eyes and ears as people jumped to their deaths. This shocking raid also included the arrest of 4,000 children.

Within a few days, detainees were transferred to one of the French concentration camps at Pithiviers, Beaune-la-Rolande or Drancy. On arrival at Beaune-la-Rolande, the children Frida, at age ten, and Roland, nine, were separated from their mother Pessa and their older sister Sara; they lived in huts with hundreds of other young children and without access to their mother. I've been unable to uncover the rationale for this unspeakable cruelty, and I can only imagine Pessa's anguish and the children's despair when they were split up.

Interned in Drancy, George Wellers testified about the camp, during the trial of Adolf Eichmann. No doubt conditions at the other camps where authorities separated children from their mothers were the same. Wellers explained that thousands of children, some as young as two, were made to sleep on "straw mattresses on the ground — mattresses which were filthy, disgusting and full of vermin ... The children arrived in very bad condition since they had already been neglected for two or three weeks at Beaune-la-Rolande and Pithiviers." Adults were not permitted to stay with the children at night, he explained, so they were "completely alone in large rooms ... in semi-darkness ... They cried, often becoming agitated as they called for their mothers. Sometimes an entire roomful of 120 children woke up in the middle of the night, out of control, screaming."[2]

At Beaune-la-Rolande, camp guards crowded approximately 200 people together in each building, where they slept on flea- and lice-ridden straw. The unhygienic living conditions caused an outbreak of diphtheria and other infectious diseases. Administrators allowed each person only a small amount of bread to eat with coffee in the morning and beans twice a day.

Pessa and Sara spent approximately two weeks in Barrack 2 at Beaune-la-Rolande before being sent together to Auschwitz on August 7, 1942, on Convoy 16. Initially, police sent children thirteen years of age and over with their parents, and at fourteen, Sara qualified to leave with her mother. The number of deportees on this convoy totalled 1,068. From this group, the Nazis gassed 794 on arrival and selected 63 men and 211 women for slave labour in Auschwitz. By 1945, a total of seven people from Convoy 16 had survived: five men and two women.

Three thousand children, including Frida and Roland, watched as their hysterical mothers departed on Convoy 16. Too young to understand but old enough to feel abandoned, most of the children did not realize that they would never see their parents again. Police held Frida and Roland at the camp for an additional two weeks before the children took their final journey to Auschwitz.

In a last-ditch effort to save the children, Mr. L. J. Eskenasy, Director of Jewish workers of the Ostland,[3] exchanged letters on August 17 and 20,

---

2. "George Wellers' Testimony about Conditions in France and Deportations from France at the Eichmann Trial, 9 May 1961,"
http://www.holocaustresearchproject.org/trials/wellers.html.
3. "Ostland" refers to the area comprising the Baltic States and parts of Poland and Belarus occupied by Germany in World War II.

1942, with Mr. Leo Israelowitz, head of the liaison service of the Union Générale des Israélites de France. Mr. Eskenasy asked Mr. Israelowitz to protect the families of Jewish workers. He specifically discussed Frida and Roland Albaum, detained in the camp of Beaune-la-Rolande, noting that their father worked in agriculture and their mother had been deported.

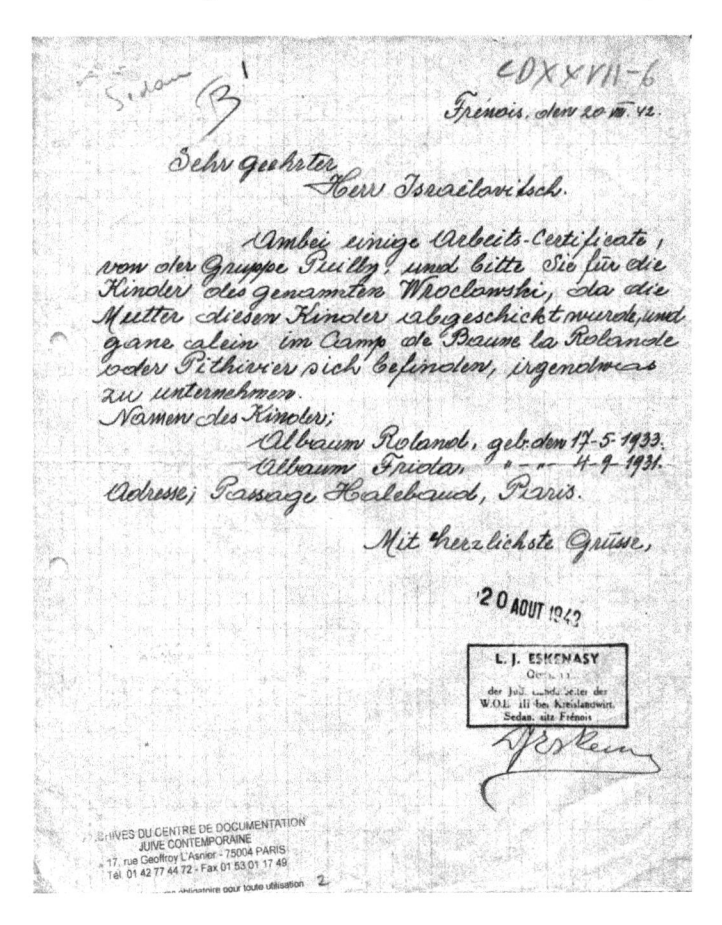

Letter from L. J. Eskenasy concerning Frida and Roland, dated August 20, 1942. (Courtesy of Mémorial de la Shoah.)

Mr. Eskenasy's efforts failed, and on August 21, 1942, authorities sent the children to Drancy in preparation for their deportation to Auschwitz. Police mixed unrelated adults with the children in each cattle car in an attempt to make the French population believe that deportees left as families. Over the course of several days, six convoys departed to

Auschwitz, each carrying five hundred children, most of whom had been arrested in the Vel d'Hiv roundup.

Wagon 3 of Convoy 22 held a total of ninety children, including Frida and Roland, along with seven adults, all of whom were strangers to one another. I will never know the fear that gripped the children when police slammed shut the door of the cattle car and locked it from the outside, plunging the interior into darkness. Being trapped inside in the heavy heat of summer with only one tiny opening for air must have been unbearable, and no doubt many of the children cried out in panic for their mothers.

Convoy 22 departed from Drancy on August 21, 1942, and arrived in Auschwitz two days later. When the doors of the cattle cars opened in Birkenau, Nazis held back snarling dogs and yelled at the terrified children, commanding them to get off the train quickly. Hundreds of adults and children, including Frida and Roland, formed lines for selection before being led to their deaths in the gas chambers of Birkenau. None of the children survived Convoy 22. Of the 1,000 deportees, Nazis gassed 892 on arrival and selected 90 men and 18 women for slave labour. By 1957 there were only seven survivors of Convoy 22, all men.

§

On August 13, 1942, the Nazis ordered the confiscation of all wireless radios from Jews in occupied France, in an effort to isolate them further and to prevent their hearing Allied broadcasts or news that could in any way assist in their survival. Then French police made a new mass arrest and detained 4,232 Jewish men in Drancy between August 20 and August 25.

While anti-Semitism within the French government continued to grow, so did concern for the Jews among some of the French clergy. The archbishop of Toulouse, Monsignor Saliège, wrote a letter to be read in the region's churches on August 23. The letter began as follows:[4]

---

4. "Pastoral Letter From His Excellency Monsignor Saliège Archbishop of Toulouse," http://www.yadvashem.org/odot_pdf/Microsoft%20Word%20-%203112.pdf.

My dearly beloved brothers,

There is a Christian morality. There is a human morality that enforces obligations and recognizes rights. These obligations and rights come from human nature. They come from God. They cannot be transgressed. No mortal has the power to abolish them. Children, women, fathers and mothers treated like a vile horde, members of the same family separated from each other and made to embark on a journey to an unknown destination ...

The letter later went on to say, pointedly, "The Jewish men are men. The Jewish women are women. The foreigners are men. The foreigners are women. None of this should be allowed to happen to them ... They are our brothers like many others. A Christian cannot forget that."

Despite confiscation of the letter by the French police on August 22, the following day clergy read Saliège's words in defiance at local churches. I would like to think that at least some of the congregants thought hard about the words contained in the letter. Certainly, it appeared that support for the government began to drop toward the end of 1942.

After the war ended several members of the Vichy government were prosecuted for their wartime activities; most notable was Marshal Pétain. However, it took the French government many years to recognize their own complicity in the deportation of more than 76,000 Jews, many of whom died in Auschwitz. Eventually, in July 1995 Jacques Chirac made a public apology for the nation's role in those deportations during World War II.

At a ceremony to commemorate the fifty-third anniversary of the roundup of over 12,000 Jews at Vel d'Hiv, Chirac called French complicity with the Nazis a stain on the nation. His speech began as follows:[5]

Mr. President, Mr. Chief Rabbi, Ladies and Gentlemen,

In the life of a nation, there are times that are painful for the memory and for one's conception of one's country.

---

5. "President Chirac addresses national ceremony in honour of Righteous of France," Speech given by M. Jacques Chirac, President of the Republic, at the national ceremony in honour of the Righteous of France in Paris, January 18, 2007, http://www.ambafrance-uk.org/President-Chirac-addresses,8745.

> It is hard to speak of these times because we sometimes struggle to find the right words to recall the horror and express the sorrow of those who lived through this tragedy: they are forever marked in their souls and in their flesh by the memory of those days of tears and shame.
>
> It is hard to speak of these times also because these dark hours have forever soiled our history, and are an insult to our past and our traditions. Yes, it is true that the criminal insanity of the occupying forces was supported by some French people and the French State.

Chirac then described "the horrible scenes" that were witnessed fifty-three years earlier: "… families torn apart, mothers separated from their children, elderly men, some of whom were veterans of the First World War and had spilled their blood for France, were callously thrown into Parisian buses and police vans …"

He went on to exhort his countrymen to be forcefully vigilant in regards to "racist and anti-Semitic ideology," because in "this domain, nothing is insignificant … Racist crimes, the defence of revisionist ideas and provocations of all kinds — little comments and quips — are all drawn from the same sources." Chirac concluded by saying, "Let us learn the lessons of history. Let us refuse to be passive onlookers, or accomplices, of the unacceptable."

Chirac's message perhaps began the healing process. But I find it difficult to forgive the betrayal of the Jews of France by their own government, an administration that not only did not protect its own citizens but also aided the enemy by trapping thousands of Jews and transporting them to their deaths.

§

I sometimes wonder if my insatiable desire for information about Benjamin borders on the obsessive. I spend hours surfing the Internet, reading books and sending out letters, and I frequently suffer from lack of sleep. I love doing the research late at night and often stay up until one or two in the morning; the house is quiet and I can concentrate without the telephone ringing and interrupting my thoughts.

I sense some uninterest from my children when I speak of every new piece of information that I uncover. Perhaps my enthusiasm occasionally consumes conversations, and I forget that they are busy with careers and child-rearing. Their lives are in the present, and for now mine is firmly planted in the past. I hope that someday all of my family will understand my motive for searching for my great-uncle: I want to elevate him from a mere number — the number tattooed on his arm in Auschwitz and his only identity at the end of his life — to Benjamin Albaum, the unique, living, breathing human being his family loved.

My mind frequently drifts to France. I think about the years that I lived in London and the summer vacations that I spent with my family driving through France, often passing through Paris on the way to Lyon and the French Riviera. What if someone in our French family had survived the war; what if it were a child?

It is late at night, and I am on my computer going through a genealogy website searching for family lost during wartime and the Holocaust. I enter the Albaum name in the search box and a new page opens with the name of someone in France looking for family by the name of Albaum. I send an email with some details about Benjamin and my family in France and Poland, not knowing if there is any connection between our relatives.

Within a few days I receive a response; Raphael Albaum, the searcher's grandfather, came from Kazanow, Poland — the same village where my great-grandparents, also Albaums, married.

His grandfather and grandmother lived in Paris prior to and during World War II and were eventually deported from France to their deaths in Majdanek and Auschwitz, respectively. Miraculously, his mother escaped the police roundups and is alive and living in France. I'm astounded and overjoyed. Kazanow is the connection for both of us, and while neither one can speculate how each fits into the family puzzle, we know we are related.

I respond immediately. We exchange phone numbers by email and speak the following day. I apologize for my poor French and then listen to his impeccable English as he reveals what he knows of his grandparents' lives and that of his mother, Céline. I call my mother, who can barely contain her excitement. Paris beckons me even more; it is time to visit. Through all the loss, I have found life!

CHAPTER 4

I glance at my watch and frown; it's four o'clock on Friday afternoon and the Mémorial de la Shoah on rue Geoffroy l'Asnier closes at 6:00 p.m. Today is the only opportunity I will have to visit the memorial. When I booked the trip to Paris, I was filled with excitement at meeting my newly-discovered cousin and her family on Sunday, completely forgetting that the museum is closed on Shabbat (Saturday).

Within minutes the taxi I'm in pulls up in front of my hotel, close to Luxembourg gardens; it oozes the European old-world charm that has drawn me to Paris in the past. I pay the driver and check into the hotel. I squeeze myself into a tiny elevator that holds one, maybe two, people at most, and it creaks and groans, slowly ascending to my floor. I try to convince myself that the elevator is safer than the stairs — I can see that the risers slant distinctly downward, a pitch that could make both ascent and descent somewhat perilous. I drop my bags in the room and take the elevator back down to the lobby.

The hotel's majestic black-and-white cat is stretched out along the edge of the front desk with front paws crossed; a large yellow Lab named Hugo is lying on the floor. Both seem unaware of the occasional passing guest. The concierge calls for a taxi and writes out directions to the Mémorial de la Shoah, where I hope to see Benjamin's name etched on the wall that commemorates the French Jewish victims of the Nazis. The taxi pulls up at the curb as I walk through the main door of the hotel, and I get into the back seat and show the driver the address. He groans in protest when he reads the location.

"*Madame — heure de pointe, vendredi après-midi à Paris!*" he yells, waving his hands in objection.

He has reminded me that not only is today Friday, it's also rush hour in Paris.

"I'm sorry, I have to get there quickly, *rapidement*," I reply.

"Okay, okay," he moans and reluctantly throws the car in gear, all the while muttering under his breath in French. We join the throng of vehicles crawling along boulevard Saint-Germain, trapped amid the cacophony of honking horns and sirens from police cars and ambulances.

The driver seems oblivious both to me and to the outside noises during the drive. The Middle Eastern music he plays on the car stereo is occasionally overshadowed by loud and animated chatter on his mobile phone. We cross the river Seine on the Pont de Sully and converge with more traffic on the Right Bank. I see the Eiffel Tower on the Champ-de-Mars in the distance; even on a dull day, Paris looks beautiful. The driver stops near the Saint Paul metro station and struggles with his GPS in a half-hearted effort to find rue Geoffroy l'Asnier. Ever more anxious about the time, I look at my watch.

"Don't worry," I say. I pay him and quickly step out of the cab, slam the door and run into a nearby wine store. I show the owner the directions. She slides her hand through my arm and walks with me to the shop door, pointing me in the right direction.

"You are very close," she says with a smile.

It is April in Paris, cold and blustery, and the heavens have let loose with a teeming rain as I rush along the cobblestone streets of the Marais. I hold my umbrella on an angle, pushing hard against the rain and wind; my other hand pulls the collar of my coat tight around my neck. I turn the corner, look up and see the street sign for rue Geoffroy l'Asnier. I hurry across the street towards the entrance to the Mémorial de la Shoah. As I shake the rain off my umbrella, I wonder how many times Benjamin walked across these streets toward his home in Saint-Ouen.

At the entrance of the building, I must go through security. After my bag is searched and X-rayed, I walk through a body scanner before I'm given clearance to proceed into the courtyard. I have only an hour to tour the building.

The museum is by no means large, but it does house various important documents over several floors. Some of the documents pertain to the deportation of the French Jews transported by the French Vichy government to Auschwitz and various other death camps during the Nazi occupation of Northern France during World War II, and others relate to the Nazis' "final solution" in which the French Jews became engulfed. The vision of these documents seems permanently embedded in my mind. I continue to grapple with the motivation and outcome of the Wannsee conference, a meeting that enabled fifteen malevolent men, while feasting on an abundance of exotic food, drinking cognac and smoking cigars, to callously orchestrate the murder of six million Jewish lives out of an intended eleven million. The list included Britain, and I shudder, knowing that I would not be here to tell this story if Germany had won the war.

I walk down the stairs to a darkened room where containers of ashes from the crematoria of each Nazi extermination camp encircle an eternal flame, burning on the floor. The room is quiet and tranquil, yet as I watch the flickering flame my eyes well with tears. Sitting on the steps looking into the room, I wipe my eyes, resolving to complete my journey in Poland, where Benjamin's life began and ended.

THE WALL OF NAMES

The names engraved on this wall are those of the 76 000 Jews, among them 11 000 children, deported from France, with the collaboration of the Vichy government, as part of the Nazi plan to exterminate Judaism in Europe. Most of them were murdered between 1942 and 1944 in Auschwitz-Birkenau, others in the Sobibor and Lublin-Maidanek camps. Only some 2 500 people survived deportation.

This wall gives an identity to the children, women and men that the Nazis tried to eradicate from the face of the earth. Their names engraved in stone, will perpetuate their memory

This long list would not be complete without the destiny of the other Jewish victims in France being associated with it :

those who died in the French internment camps (more than 2 200 died, in particular in Gurs, Pithiviers, Beaune-la-Rolande and Drancy), those shot as hostages or summarily slaughtered by the Nazis and their French auxiliaries, those who disappeared, whose fate remains unknown, the resistance fighters and rescuers who died while on assignments or in Nazi concentration camps.

Nearly 6 millions Jews living in Europe were assassinated by the Nazis during the Second World War.

« Zakhor, we will remember »

Photo I took of the Wall of Names at the Mémorial de la Shoah, Paris.

I make my way up the stairs and out of the building to the grey stone walls etched with the names of thousands and thousands of Jews deported by the French government and murdered in Auschwitz and other extermination camps at the hands of the Nazis. Although I've received information from the Shoah Memorial about Benjamin, I'm not sure if his name has made it onto the wall. Victims are listed alphabetically and in a short time I do find Benjamin Albaum. I trace my finger over his name and I want to hug the wall; just seeing his name makes me feel closer to him. I am frantic to find a stone, a pebble, anything that I can place on the ground below his name because it is customary to leave a stone at the grave of a loved one when visiting a Jewish cemetery.

```
...IONAS 1910 • Esther AKRICHE 1907 • Zelda AKRICHE 1901
884 • Szmaja AKSELRAD 1896 • Joseph AKSENHAUS 1928
aham ALALOF 1895 • Robert ALALOF 1918 • Haïm ALALOUF 1905
• Alfred ALBAN • Aaron ALBAUM 1905 • Benjamin ALBAUM 1905
Aron ALBERT 1907 • Isaac ALBERT 1890 • Jeannette ALBERT 1925
lathan ALBERT 1890 • Ojwa ALBERT 1898 • Rachel ALBERT 1870
OHAIRR 1907 • Isaac ALBOUHAIR 1908 • Esther ALCABES 1878
```

Photo I took of Benjamin Albaum's name on the Wall of Names at the Mémorial de la Shoah, Paris.

This long-standing tradition possibly originated in ancient times when mourners placed the dead directly into the ground and covered the body with dirt and large stones. It is believed that family members would return periodically to place more stones on the grave, not only to secure the site but also to bring them emotionally closer to their departed loved one by showing that a visitor had been there. Eventually, carved headstones became the norm, but the custom of leaving a small piece of rock, a pebble or stone on top of the headstone after every visit has continued to the present.

Today I want to show that someone from Benjamin's family has been here. But I find nothing suitable to mark my visit, and the building will soon close. All I can do before I leave is stand in the damp cold and retrace Benjamin's name with my finger one more time. Tears fill my eyes again and roll down my face, stinging my cold cheeks. I leave the museum and promise myself that I will return one day to place a candle and a stone beneath Benjamin's name.

A Stone for Benjamin

> D 1894 • Chaïm AKTOR 1905 • Marie AKTOR 1930 • Rachel AKTOR 1940 • Zelda AKTOR 190
> 92 • Samuel ALATON 1903 • Rachel ALBA 1886 • Joseph ALBAGLI 1899 • Mayer ALBAHAR
> 31 • Pessa ALBAUM 1913 • Rolande ALBAUM 1933 • Rose ALBAUM 1914 • Sara ALBAUM
> 5 • Julius ALBERT 1871 • Marie ALBERT 1902 • Martha ALBERT 1893 • Mordka ALBERT 1
> 1876 • Chava ALBERTE 1894 • Siegfried ALBIN 1873 • Joseph ALBOHAIR 1888 • Salomo
> 1899 • Samuel ALCALAY 1892 • Behar ALCAMZI 1893 • Elise ALCHEK 1897 • Albert AL

Photo I took of Pessa, Sara and Roland's names on the Wall of Names at the Mémorial de la Shoah, Paris. Roland's name has an e *on the end; it was probably copied from the Convoy 22 documents, where it was also misspelled.*

No longer in a hurry, I think about taking the metro back to my hotel, but a taxi is parked on the street outside Saint Paul station, and I jump in. Unlike the drive here, the journey back to the Left Bank is fast. My driver is pleasant and he points out some interesting sights along the way. I ask him to stop at the corner of rue Saint-Germaine, close to my hotel.

I look up at the sky; the sun is setting behind the dissipating rain clouds that hung over Paris during the afternoon. I'm cold, tired and hungry, and I walk over to a vendor on the street corner. He prepares a fresh cheese crepe for me and wraps it in a paper cone. Walking the short distance back to the hotel, I bite into my crepe, and warm steam evaporates into the damp, early-evening air. As I stroll the narrow street, I try to process everything that I have just seen.

The front door of the hotel is welcoming. I pick up my room key from the desk clerk, pat Hugo, the dog, and take the elevator up to the third floor. Once in my room, I kick off my shoes, lie back on the bed and close my eyes. The image that stays with me is Benjamin's name etched on the grey stone wall.

Saturday morning I get a ticket to the Musée d'Orsay. The museum is situated on the Seine opposite the Tuileries Garden, and I spend hours wandering through the art exhibitions and viewing my favourite Monets, Manets and Van Goghs. I have lunch at a charming café and spend the afternoon browsing stores. Bulbs are in bloom everywhere, and despite the cool temperature, the sun is bright and Paris looks like spring.

My cousin has invited me to lunch on Sunday at her son's home in the Paris suburbs, so I stop at a busy chocolatier, where I select a small box full of handmade bonbons to bring to Céline and her family. On Saturday evening, my dinner with champagne is delicious at a restaurant near the Eiffel Tower, which glows in its nighttime splendour. I return to the hotel and fall asleep looking forward to the next day, when I will meet my new French family for the first time.

I have arranged to meet Céline outside the train station. Several people are waiting there, yet somehow we recognize each other and immediately hug. Céline drives us to her son's home, where I am warmly welcomed by him, his wife and their young children. I hand Céline a gift; it is a framed photograph of my great-grandfather Szulima Albaum and his family in Poland, which I copied and brought with me from Toronto. We all chat in both English and French and enjoy a delicious homemade lunch of hearty beef casserole with salad, followed by a sumptuous flan for dessert and a wonderful French cheese to finish.

There is so much to tell them about the Albaum family, and I realize how fortunate I am that my grandmother and mother passed on the family stories. At this point I know very little of Céline's story, though her son has told me that she became an orphan at a very young age. I look at her and admire her strength for having survived what must have been terrible loneliness and despair. It is obvious that she is beloved by her family, and the mutual adoration between Céline and her grandchildren is palpable.

Sadly, I have to leave in time to catch the Eurostar back to London. Céline insists on travelling with me on the train to the Gare du Nord. We talk constantly about our lives, and in spite of her broken English and my poor French, we are able to understand one another. Between this conversation and later emails, I am able to piece together more of her story.

Céline, an only child, became an orphan at the age of four after police deported her parents from France to their deaths in Majdanek and Auschwitz.

"After the death of my parents," Céline tells me, "I felt like an object that could be moved around by adults at a whim, never knowing where and with whom I would be living from one day to the next." Even at such an early age she remembers feeling desperately alone, as though she were living in a nightmare with none of her family to watch over and love her. Like Céline, many Jewish children in France — estimated at between 5,000 and 15,000 — lost their parents during the war. Some of these children became role models for her and a bulwark against the loneliness she felt.

Within days of the war ending, officials established an office in Paris to gather information and to defend the legal and property rights of abandoned and orphaned children. Authorities created organizations, such as the Oeuvre de Protection des Enfants Juifs and the Oeuvre de Secours aux Enfants, as well as children's homes, summer camps, vocational centres and medical facilities specifically to care for the orphaned children.

A French Jewish couple adopted Céline when she was seven years old. "They showered me with love and affection," she recalls, but despite their efforts, she constantly yearned for her parents to return even though she knew that it was impossible.

When Céline turned fourteen, her adoptive father died, and all her feelings of abandonment, never far from the surface, returned in spades. Céline's adoptive mother became seriously depressed after her husband died, and again Céline felt empty and deserted. "But fortunately," she tells me, over the muted clacking of the train wheels, "when I joined the youth organization Hachomer Hatzaïr, I learned that I could be myself among the friends I made there."

After spending some time on a kibbutz in Israel, Céline returned to France, got married and had two children. Though her marriage did not last, her children helped create the sense of family that had been missing in her life for so many years.

Now that I know Céline's story, I think about how different her childhood might have been had my grandparents and parents known of her survival. I look over at my new-found cousin and she's smiling. In spite of all her losses, I realize that Céline's love of life has never really left her.

The train pulls into the Gare du Nord and we get out, climb some stairs and walk toward the platform where I will get on the train departing for London.

We turn and hug each other in a tearful goodbye. I don't want to let her go. Life can be cruel; Céline has spent most of her life without relatives from the Albaum family, and now that we have found each other, it is difficult to part. I hug her again and we promise to always stay in touch with each other. I clear immigration, scan my bags at customs, walk onto the platform and turn. Céline is still standing in the place I left her, and we wave at each other one more time as I step aboard the carriage.

The train eases out of the station and gradually picks up speed as we head toward the tunnel that connects France with England. The carriage sways from side to side as the wheels race along the rails during the two-and-a-half-hour journey back to London. I relax in my seat, alternately dozing and staring out the window while reflecting on the three days I have just spent in Paris. Visiting the Mémorial de la Shoah has made the death of Benjamin real, but it is not enough for me. I need to know the facts surrounding his death in Auschwitz, and I resolve to continue with my research after I return home.

§

Once back in Toronto, I call my parents as soon as the plane lands. There is so much to tell them, but between the long flight and the jet lag, all I want to do is go home, have a snack and go to bed. I promise to visit them later the next day.

I open my eyes and look at the clock: it is 4:00 a.m. I try going back to sleep but my mind is too active. It will take a few days for my body to adjust to the five-hour time change. I lie in bed for an hour listening to the birds singing their dawn chorus. I have to get up; I'm wide awake.

I make some tea, turn on the computer and run a search on the Auschwitz website for Albaum, not anticipating any information since the Nazis destroyed the majority of the camp records just prior to the liberation of the camp in 1945. A new page opens; it contains partially preserved records for "Albaum, Benjam. [sic] B.1905-01-15, camp serial number: 48883." The birthdate is the same as Uncle Benjamin's, but there is no date of death, and my mind starts racing with what-ifs. I download the information and send off a letter by regular mail requesting more details from the archives in Auschwitz.

Several months later, a response arrives in the mail from Auschwitz. Benjamin Albaum, prisoner number 48883, died on May 21, 1943. I read the letter and think how cold and matter of fact its contents are. By changing the identity of someone from a name to a number, one feels disconnected from that person, a once-living, once-breathing human being. The Nazis shaved Benjamin's head, issued him prison-striped clothing and tattooed the number 48883 on his arm. Each individual became a number. The prisoners all looked the same and psychologically lost their identities, which is exactly what the Nazis wanted.

Now I am beginning to understand what is driving my obsession: every piece of information about Benjamin that I gather helps negate the Nazi doctrine of dehumanizing their victims. I want to erase the idea of Benjamin as a number. He should be remembered as a human being, a man with feelings and a man who loved life and cared deeply for his wife and children. I want to give Benjamin back his life.

CHAPTER 5

I open the patio door on an early summer morning in 2006, and the sun warms my face while I sip tea and read *The Globe & Mail*. An article by Susan Sachs catches my eye: "In a landmark ruling, French court holds national railway accountable for wartime deportations by Nazis ..." I run a search on Google and find several more stories about France's national state-owned railway corporation, including one from the British newspaper, the *Guardian*. The headline states, "French state and SNCF guilty of collusion in deporting Jews," and the article begins as follows:[6]

> In a historic judgment, the French state and the state railway company SNCF were found guilty yesterday of colluding in the deportation of Jews during the Second World War and ordered to pay compensation to the family of two victims.
>
> The Green MEP [member of the European Parliament] Alain Lipietz and his sister, Hélène, brought the case on behalf of their [deceased] father, who was transported from Toulouse to the Drancy wartime transit camp outside Paris. It is the latest embarrassment for France, which for decades refused to face up to accusations of collaboration in the Holocaust during the Nazi occupation.

The story goes on to mention the amount paid in compensation to the family (£43,000) and notes "the judges found that the SNCF railway company never voiced 'any objections' about transporting such prisoners," even though "the state could not 'obviously' ignore the fact that transportation to Drancy would normally mean subsequent removal to a Nazi death camp." The article also quotes Mr. Lipietz as saying, "It's the

---

6. Angelique Chrisafis, "French state and SNCF guilty of collusion in deporting Jews," *The Guardian*, June 7, 2006.

first time in history that the state and the SNCF have, as such, been condemned."

Could it be that the SNCF is finally being held responsible for their complicity with the Nazis? Haunted by thoughts of my family members in those cattle cars, I go to my computer and research lawyers involved in the case. Class action lawsuits are already underway in the United States. Because France allows class action lawsuits only from outside the country, Avi Bitton, a Parisian lawyer, is representing numerous claimants against the SNCF, all with petitions similar to that of the Lipietz family.

I telephone my father, who answers the phone in his usual cheerful voice.

"I just came across an article in the paper," I tell him. "The SNCF has been found guilty of collusion in the deportation of Jews during the war."

"Really?" He sounds surprised.

"Dad," I say, "other families are petitioning the French government and the SNCF, and I think we should too. But we need to discuss this with Mom first."

It's not about the money, of course; we both recognize that. It's about justice.

I can almost hear him thinking.

"Yes, you're absolutely right," he says at last, "but first we have to tell her everything we know about Benjamin, including his death."

I tell him I'll drop by their house at my usual time later that afternoon.

§

"Mom," I say, "I have some news."

We are sitting in the living room again. My father and I gently tell my mother, without giving her any concrete details, that we now have proof that Benjamin is dead. Our words confirm what she already suspected; at least we now have the exact date of his death and can light a remembrance candle for him on each anniversary.

Then I tell her about the SNCF. I explain that North American–style class action lawsuits are not permissible within France because each claimant must be individually named in the lawsuit and each claim must be heard separately, making petitions a lengthy process. Still, my mother wants to see this case before the French courts. After much discussion, she asks me to retain Avi Bitton and make a claim on behalf of Benjamin and his family.

After extensive telephone calls with Avi, I commence an action on behalf of my family against the SNCF and the State of France for their complicity in the deaths of Benjamin, Pessa, Sara, Frida and Roland Albaum and the deaths of Benjamin's sister Chava, her husband, their five children and an unmarried cousin, Aaron Albaum.

Avi calls me in Toronto and asks if I'll speak with journalists regarding the case. I agree but only if I can speak anonymously. I explain that I represent my family and I don't want my mother to receive potentially harassing phone calls from journalists or anyone else, given her age and poor health.

The phone is ringing; a journalist from CanWest News Service introduces himself. He wants to interview me regarding my case against the SNCF and the State of France. Avi has already told him I wish to remain anonymous. He has agreed to my terms and conducts the interview over the phone. The *National Post* prints the story by Randy Boswell on August 30, 2006, under the headline "French Railway Threatened with Lawsuit over Holocaust." A few days later I'm contacted by the BBC in London to set up a telephone interview with Jonathan Charles for his BBC World News program, *Crossing Continents*. Through Benjamin's death I have become an advocate for him, and a voice within me needs to make the world aware of what happened to the Jews in France during World War II. Finally, I notice a letter in the *Canadian Jewish News* entitled "Canadians seek French redress for Auschwitz transports," on October 5, 2006, written by Michael R. Marrus, co-author of *Vichy France and the Jews*. Marrus's letter disagrees with the growing litigation against the SNCF because he does not believe that the courts are the place to discuss history. But for me the case is not about history, it is about facts: France sent 76,000 Jews to their deaths on SNCF trains. Our family is looking for an acknowledgement from the SNCF of their complicity in these deaths, including the death of Benjamin Albaum, and whether historians agree or disagree with the case strikes me as irrelevant.

A few days later I respond with an emailed letter to the editor and sign it with a pseudonym. I receive a response from the paper; they want to publish my letter but refuse to print it without proper attribution. I initially refuse, but eventually I agree to let them print my real name. My letter is published on November 16, 2006, under the heading "French Auschwitz transports":

> The Société nationale des chemins de fer français (SNCF) case is about how the railway transported Jews during the Nazi Occupation of France throughout World War II. There is no question that the SNCF used livestock cars for the transportation of Jews to death camps such as Auschwitz.
>
> In 1997, French President Jacques Chirac recognized France's role in the oppression of Jews during World War II, and the subsequent trial of Maurice Papon, a French Vichy government official who collaborated with the Nazis, proved the undeniable participation of the government and therefore its agencies in the deportations. While the SNCF may argue that the German and the French governments called the shots, they have not provided proof that they were forced by any entity to charge a fare for a service they did not supply.
>
> In the Lipietz case, in which Alain Lipietz and his sister successfully sued the railway and the French government, three judges debated on the liability of the SNCF for five years and examined the exhibits produced by the SNCF and by the plaintiffs. How can French historians challenge such a judgement when they have never had access to the SNCF's archives?
>
> My uncle fought in the French army from 1939 to 1940. He was one of the earlier detainees brought in to custody and was sent to Pithiviers on May 14, 1941. He was deported to Auschwitz on July 17, 1942, and, according to infirmary records, died in Auschwitz on May 21, 1943, the same month that Josef Mengele arrived at the camp. In total, thirteen members of our Paris family — including seven children — were interned in Pithiviers and Drancy and then deported to their deaths.
>
> Whether historians agree or disagree [on the validity of litigation with the SNCF] is irrelevant. If any group has a right to be apoplectic, it is the survivors and families of those who lost their lives, either during or after their sub-human transportation on the SNCF cattle cars.

Avi asks me if I am willing to go to France to testify on behalf of my family should the case go to trial, and I agree. The more I uncover about the complicity of France and the SNCF in the death of Benjamin, the more resolute I become in pursuing justice in his name.

Ultimately the Lipietz case is overturned in February 2009 when the Conseil d'état, France's administrative court, overturns the earlier 2006 court ruling against the SNCF. I am disappointed at this news, because a precedent may have been set, and pursuing the matter now looks futile. But at least our cases have helped expose, outside of the history books, the facts surrounding the deportations of French Jews.

On a trip to the United States in November 2010, the SNCF's chief executive Guillaume Pépy releases the first public statement from the corporation on the matter. In it he says that the company wishes "to convey its profound sorrow and regret" for its actions during World War II. Given the SNCF's steadfast rejection of complicity in the deportation of Jews from France during the war, the statement comes as a surprise. The SNCF is eager to win contracts worth billions of dollars to build high-speed rail links in the US at this time, but lawmakers in California, Maryland and Florida have clearly stipulated that companies that do not acknowledge their wartime roles in deportations cannot bid on the contracts. California introduces bill 619 requiring all rail companies bidding on high-speed contracts to fully disclose their Holocaust activities; however, the bill is rejected by then–Governor Schwarzenegger.

Although the SNCF opened its files to historian Christian Bachelier in 1992, it took eight years for the report to be printed in French and wasn't made available to the public until the year 2000. The company claims that it has commissioned a translator to transcribe the report into English. However, more than twenty years have passed since Bachelier began his review of the SNCF records and, as of 2013, the English edition has yet to be published.

Secrecy creates suspicion, and though the SNCF have continued to vigorously defend their actions through litigation, a cloud still hangs over the company as to their complicity with the Nazis during World War II. The SNCF maintains that their archives are open to the public, but while arrangements can be made to view documents in their archives, photocopying of documents is forbidden. In 2012, the SNCF turned over digital copies of its archives to three Holocaust museums.

Sadly, it has taken over sixty-five years and the inability for the company to bid on multi-billion-dollar contracts in the US for the SNCF to acknowledge any regret for their actions during World War II. And although the SNCF may have expressed regret, the corporation has not accepted any responsibility for the deaths of vast numbers of French Jews, including Benjamin and his family.

Yet out of all of this, one more small but precious fact emerges for me. In doing further research for my family's lawsuit, I receive another copy of Benjamin's arrest record from the Shoah Memorial. This time they've included a page I hadn't seen before, a section for descriptions of distinguishing features. Two of the notations are impossible to read because the document is too dark, but this I can decipher: his hair colour is listed as *noir* — black — and his eye colour as *marine*, or deep blue. Now whenever I look at Benjamin's photograph, I see his eyes as blue. And though my eyes are brown, my mother's eyes are also deep blue, and so, amazingly, are those of my youngest grandchild.

CHAPTER 6

Benjamin's life took many twists and turns and I have already followed him to France. It is now time to see the places where Benjamin's life began and ended. It takes more than a year to plan my itinerary and arrange for a knowledgeable and reliable guide, but I am now ready to visit Poland.

My mother's health is deteriorating and I hold back from booking my flight until the last minute out of fear of leaving her. She has fallen at home and is in hospital with fractured ribs. Yet to see the sparkle in her eyes and hear her say the Yiddish phrase *a Leben ahf dein kop* (a blessing on your head) when I speak of each new piece of information about the family, I realize if I want to bring back photographs so she can see the villages and towns where my grandparents were born and lived that it is now or never.

It is a beautiful spring morning in May 2007. The plane taxis down the runway in Toronto gaining momentum; the nose rises into the air as we lift off the ground, climbing in altitude and turning east toward England. I will be away for nine days and quietly pray to myself that my mother's health does not get worse while I am gone.

From Heathrow I travel to Gatwick, and though I am not early, I am one of only a handful of passengers waiting for the flight. Eventually travellers flying to Kraków make their way through the hustle and bustle of the awaking airport and take seats near the gate. Plump, harried British business people speak officiously on their mobile phones or tap out emails on their BlackBerrys. Gaunt Polish nationals dressed in drab colours wait with expressionless faces; none of these people smile, laugh or even frown. With lips hardly moving, they quietly exchange words with travelling companions.

When it's finally time to board, the muscles in my stomach tighten in both anticipation and trepidation at the thought of seeing the birthplace of not only my grandparents but also Benjamin. Despite all my planning,

I'm nervous at the thought of travelling alone in a country still adjusting to democracy after communism and still living with the pervasive stigma of the Holocaust.

As I tighten my seat belt, I question my judgment. Why am I visiting Poland at this time, knowing the risks of leaving my mother in such a frail state? But deep down I have always yearned to walk in my grandparents' footsteps on the streets of Skaryszew, where Sheva carried pails of water from the well to her home. I long to stand on the riverbank of the Vistula in Lublin, where Moshe Aron waded, taking a short cut to the yeshiva with his Hebrew books on his head to keep them dry. Most of all I want to stand tall in Auschwitz and light a candle in memory of Benjamin Albaum and all the other members of the family murdered by the Nazis.

Passengers settle into their seats, flight attendants secure the doors and the plane gently pushes back from the gate before we taxi to the runway. I sit in a window seat hoping to catch a glimpse of the scenery as we cross the English Channel and fly over France and Germany, but the cloud cover is relentless and I doze for most of the journey. When we begin our descent in Kraków my stomach knots again, this time in excitement as I anticipate scenery I have imagined but never seen. I peer out of the window when the plane banks and breaks through the clouds. All I can see are quiet country roads cutting through emerald green rolling hills. Fields are lush and horses graze peacefully in the bucolic landscape. It is a stark contrast to the circumstances sixty-five years earlier when Nazis surrounded terrified Polish Jews, some of them my family, who struggled to flee their assailants.

My mind returns to the present when the tires of the plane screech on the runway, and I join the throng of people in the terminal building waiting to be processed by immigration. Kraków is unseasonably hot and muggy, and the slow pace of the immigration agents exacerbates my discomfort. Finally I reach the immigration officer, a handsome young Polish man, tall, with blond hair and blue eyes, but his face is expressionless as he scrutinizes my passport. He turns the pages slowly then flips each one back and forth several times. After what seems like an interminable period of time, and with much handwringing, sweating and huddling with colleagues, he finally stamps my passport. With a sense of relief, I wish him *nostrovia (good health)* and for a moment I think he almost smiles.

I grab my bag and head through the exit doors, praying that my guide is still waiting for me. Tomasz is anxiously holding up a card with my handwritten name on it and I'm relieved to see him standing there. Any apprehensions I may have had about travelling alone diminish the moment Tomasz holds out his hand and warmly greets me.

Tomasz insists on carrying my suitcase, and as we walk the short distance toward his car in the parking lot, I notice he has an understated self-confidence despite his relatively young age and I am immediately at ease. It takes about half an hour to drive into the city of Kraków, and I take no notice of the scenery. My mind drifts to the past again when we discuss my itinerary and touch on the tumultuous history of Poland and its Jews.

"Tomasz," I say, "I never asked you this when we were emailing about my trip, but how did you come to be so interested in Jewish Poland?"

He tells me that both his parents graduated as chemists, but no one had any choices under Communism, and the government sent his parents to work in a chemical factory in Oświęcim. "And that is where we lived."

"You grew up in the shadow of Auschwitz?" I ask, a bit surprised.

Eyes on the road, he nods. "Knowing the importance of Auschwitz in Polish history, my father took me to the camp when I was thirteen, but I came away not really understanding the significance of what had happened there. You have to remember that during the rule of Communism the Polish government tightly controlled various levels of education. Under the watchful eye of the Soviet Union, our schools did not teach the complete history of World War II or the Holocaust, so I had no previous knowledge to relate to."

When he was eighteen, though, and following in his parents' footsteps studying chemistry, a friend suggested that they visit Auschwitz together and really explore the camp.

"Seeing Auschwitz through adult eyes really changed me," he says, "so much so that I switched my major to history." Tomasz goes on to tell me that after learning English, he went to Israel to take courses on the Holocaust. "Now I am working on my PhD, and I hope to teach Jewish history at the university level in Poland someday."

"But you are not Jewish, right?" I am guessing here, but his name seems an unusual one for a Polish Jew.

"No I'm not," he replies. "All of my family are Catholic."

I tell him I admire him for following his heart and that not everyone could or would do what he has done. Tomasz goes on to fill me in on some history of the Jews in Poland, and I envy his vast knowledge of the subject.

We drive directly to the hotel in Kraków and I quickly check in. The clerk speaks perfect English and is agreeable if a trifle aloof. I have purposely chosen not to stay in a traditional Polish hotel. Most are close to the huge market square in Kraków, and though the facades look appealing with their old-world charm, they have also been known to have unreliable plumbing and thin windowpanes that do little to stop the noise of late night revellers leaving pubs and restaurants. Given my short but intense stay, I want to make sure that I am able to sleep at night. My room is pleasant with just a hint of Polish influence, and the hotel is within easy walking distance of the vast market square.

It is 1:00 p.m., and fatigue and disorientation are beginning to creep over me. I try to refresh myself by splashing cool water on my face, but Tomasz is waiting for me in the front lobby of the hotel and there's no time now for repose. I'm relieved when he suggests that we drive instead of walk to the Jewish Old Town to begin my tour of Kraków.

Still hot and sticky from an early hint of summer, we eat lunch outside on the patio of one of the restaurants in the old Jewish area. When I realize that haute cuisine is not part of Polish culture, I opt for a chicken Caesar salad, which turns out to be one of the better meals that I eat in Poland. Several small eateries dot the cobblestone square, many of them trying to replicate the Jewish signs and decor reminiscent of a lost era and culture. Interiors are small, dark and dingy, with wood plank floors and wooden tables and chairs. Candles glow in tall polished brass candlestick holders on tables beside windows. The menus feature traditional Jewish-style food, but as I discover later, none of the foods come close to the taste, aromas and flavours of the traditional Jewish fare that I know.

Kraków's only emotional attachment for me is the probability that some members of my family may have passed through there, crammed into a cattle car with hundreds of other Jews on their way to their deaths in Auschwitz. But Kraków is filled with architecturally-beautiful old buildings and a sense of a long forgotten way of life. Many of today's descendants of the Ashkenazi Jews of Eastern Europe come from Hasidic backgrounds, and I instantly feel a certain sense of belonging when I view remnants of what had obviously been a thriving Jewish community.

We visit the few synagogues that still stand in the Jewish Old Town and other parts of the city. A sense of humility sweeps over me as I enter each building. Simple structures built without the grandiosity we see in the modern designs of North American synagogues and temples, these are buildings that reflect the pious purity of Judaism. It is here that I begin to sense the enormity of the loss, not only in lives but of a culture and a way of life that can never be replicated.

Beside the Remuh Synagogue is the old Jewish cemetery. As soon as I walk through the gate I'm struck by an unusual sight: nearly all the headstones — some hundreds of years old — are covered at the very top with a metal cap in an effort to protect the stone monuments from further erosion. Most of the caps have small stones sitting on them, left by people who visited, and I feel a pang remembering that I was not able to leave a pebble for Benjamin at the Shoah memorial.

Tomasz drops me off at the hotel in the late afternoon. I am worn out after almost two days of travelling and an afternoon of sightseeing. I flop down in the tub chair beside the desk and call room service to order a sandwich and a large pot of tea. I want to have an early night. Tomasz will pick me up from the hotel early in the morning, and plans to drive several hundred kilometers tomorrow on our journey to Lublin via Radom, Skaryszew, Kazanow, Pulawy and Kazimierz Dolny.

The tea tastes delicious and I end up drinking the entire pot while I exchange brief email messages with my family in London and Toronto. I assure them I am well, while the Toronto contingent reassure me that my mother is comfortable and stable in hospital and my father is coping.

I climb into bed between the cool, crisp, white sheets and I'm filled with emotion. Under the soft feather duvet, I'm a mixture of excitement and anticipation along with a touch of apprehension. I reflect on my grandmother Sheva (short for Bathsheva) who, without any desire to speak Polish or return to Poland again, left Skaryszew to join my grandfather in England; on the other hand my grandfather Morris (Moshe Aron) longed to revisit Lublin, his childhood home, before he died but never did. My thoughts drift further to Sheva's baby brother, Benjamin. Each of these people had the courage to leave their close-knit Hasidic families in Poland for what they hoped would be a better life. And now I'm not only going to see Skaryszew, the birthplace of my grandmother and her siblings, but also Auschwitz, where the Nazis murdered Benjamin.

The uneasiness I sense that night continues throughout my entire journey in Poland, and I find the contradiction curious: I have such feelings of trepidation, but I still want to see more. I never knew Benjamin but I feel him in my heart, and each time I discover new information about him, I look at his photograph and his face becomes alive. It is with those paradoxical thoughts that I drift into restless sleep.

§

I awake the next morning revived and refreshed eager to start the day. Breakfast turns out to be very good, with numerous dishes catering to guests of various nationalities. I meet Tomasz in the lobby; he loads my luggage into his car, and then we are off. Traffic is crawling through Kraków, but Tomasz handles rush hour with proficiency and calm while dodging trams and pedestrians. Driving in Krakow is similar to the rest of Europe's traffic chaos, and fortunately almost all the cars are small, allowing what North Americans would consider diabolical manoeuvres. Remarkably, there are few traffic accidents, at least while I am there.

We plan to reach Radom by lunch time after driving north east, approximately 185 kilometres from Kraków. As soon as we join the road to Radom, the traffic gains momentum, and the nonstop conversation between Tomasz and me makes the time pass quickly. During this leg of the journey, Tomasz begins educating me in the history of the Polish Jews and the difficulties that they faced.

"It is believed that the first Jewish settlers came from Spain by way of Germany and Bohemia," Tomasz says. They appeared in Poland between 800 and 900 CE (Common Era) and traded with Slovak tribes, primarily in furs and fabrics including silk.

Tomasz goes on to explain that in the thirteenth century, Jews were given the freedom to trade goods and conduct their own financial transactions in some parts of Poland. Eventually, ethnic riots broke out and Jews were required to live in areas away from the general population. During the sixteenth century, new laws were passed restricting Jews from living in several towns. By then many Jews were forced to live on the outside of shtetls (villages). Poland's borders were frequently changing, a fact that also negatively affected the rights of Jews.

World War II broke out when Germany invaded Poland in 1939. There were well over three million Jews living in Poland. The Nazis isolated the Jews in ghettos. Work was difficult to find and so was food. Many died in the ghettos of starvation and disease. Some Jews were taken out in groups, shot by Nazi firing squads and buried in mass graves. Then gassings began, first in trucks with carbon monoxide, but ultimately, millions were sent to the gas chambers at Auschwitz, Majdanek, Treblinka and other extermination camps that were mainly located in Poland.

By the end of the war, the Nazis had murdered more than three million Polish Jews. Anti-Semitism continued in Poland after the war ended, and the few thousand Jews there who had survived the war left the country during the ensuing years.

In the year 2000, a mere 3,500 Jews lived in Poland, but according to the World Jewish Congress, approximately 5,000 Jews live there today. Poland now has a Chief Rabbi, and as the country continues to grow its democracy in the post-Communist era, young Poles are showing a keen interest in the history of Polish Jews. Some of them are beginning to ask questions about their heritage and discovering that one or both of their parents or grandparents are Jewish.

Tomasz then describes to me the Jewish Cultural Festival that attracts Jewish musicians, actors, and writers from Israel and around the world to Krakow each year. They perform for thousands of Poles and visitors in celebration of the Jewish culture that was once commonplace in cities and towns throughout Poland.

§

Tomasz and I approach Radom, making our first stop at the main Jewish cemetery, situated beside a commercial business. Several headstones are still standing but the rusted metal gates are locked. Tomasz sets off to locate the key, which is often held by a local resident. A wild goose chase ensues as he is sent from place to place, but the key is never located, and we are both disappointed.

We make our way back to the centre of town and park the car. Both of us are hungry, and we decide to grab some lunch before continuing on to some of the important buildings in Radom. I take in some of the sights as we stroll down Żeromskiego Street, an attractive, pedestrian-friendly road closed to traffic. It takes a while to find a restaurant. Tomasz explains that there are not many choices in smaller towns because Poles are not used to going out to eat; most families can't afford the expense. Finally we find a cafe serving Greek food, but since I don't recognize most of the food on the menu, I order a salad. I chuckle to myself as the owner and waiter repeatedly look across at Tomasz and me with approving smiles. The owner makes gestures and suggests in Polish that Tomasz give me the small bunch of flowers from the vase on the table; Tomasz blushes, obviously embarrassed. Little does the waiter know that not only are we married to different people, I am old enough to be Tomasz's mother.

We leave the restaurant and walk back to the main square. Beautiful buildings, including St. Stanislaus Garrison Church have been refurbished, but the formerly Jewish area bears no resemblance to its vibrant past. Tomasz points to the bustling municipal offices across the street that served as the Radom Nazi headquarters during the war.

My mind slips back to 1939 and I picture uniformed SS officers hurriedly coming and going. I wonder if this is the building where the Albaums registered for their ghetto passes and received their fateful yellow stars.

Set up by the Germans in 1941 the Radom ghetto housed more than 30,000 Jews; some came from the city and others from outlying villages including Skaryszew and Kazanow. The Nazis murdered almost all the Jews by firing squad or sent them to the death camp of Treblinka before liquidating the Radom ghetto, deporting the last surviving residents to Auschwitz in July 1944.

I feel a chill on my back, unsure if I'm responding to my thoughts of the Radom ghetto Jews or am simply cold. As my mind returns to the present I realize that the temperature is falling and I left my coat at the hotel in Kraków.

I button up my sweater to stay warm while we hurry back to the car. Anticipation takes over as we make the fourteen-kilometer drive to

Skaryszew, the birth place of my grandmother, Benjamin and their siblings.

I have no preconceived ideas about how the villages and towns will appear, but I hope that Skaryszew in particular will have some unique characteristics along its roads and avenues. We drive into the little town and park the car at the cobblestone market square. Surrounding the square are small row houses without any particularly interesting features though some look extremely old. I walk around the square and stand under some large old trees. I know that my great-grandmother sold fruits and vegetables here, and my great-grandparents, grandmother and her sisters and brothers had all walked across the cobblestone roads that surround the square.

Tomasz stops two older men and asks them in Polish if they remember any of the Jewish families who once lived there. They nod their heads while describing recollections of lining up outside Jewish homes to receive the non-kosher food the Jews gave away at Passover. Suddenly Tomasz stops translating for me. He takes my arm and leads me away. I ask him what's wrong; he is reluctant at first to tell me but I insist.

Tomasz looks back at the men and then says, "They told me that they would help light the fires for the Jews on Shabbat, and they said that when it was time to bake the matzos for Passover, the Jews used the blood of Christian children to make the dough." Tomasz is clearly uncomfortable, and I'm taken aback that people still repeat blood libel, anti-Semitic cock-and-bull stories. The two old men, who repeated these lies, laugh at us as we cross the street, obviously enjoying their game.

Tomasz shakes his head and says, in an effort to reassure me, "The old people still remember the stories from the past, but the young Poles are different, especially since the end of communism. We are educated and have the freedom to travel and read books. We don't listen to those old stories."

It is the only anti-Semitic incident that I experience in Poland but one that I will not forget.

Tomasz and I walk toward the small bank built on the former site of the once-thriving synagogue. There is no trace of the yeshiva that Benjamin attended. A short walk down the unpaved road behind the bank stands an old well that the Jews of Skayrszew used.

"I wonder how many times my grandmother dipped her bucket in the water here and carried it back to her home," I say to Tomasz. I wish my mother were here now. We drive to the outskirts of the town and find the site of what used to be the Jewish cemetery. Again, anticipation churns my stomach; I am hoping I might find my great-grandparents' headstone, but there is nothing to see other than overgrown trees, bushes and vines. I look back to the town, which is within walking distance of this former cemetery, and visualize funeral processions of the Jews of Skaryszew. There are no monuments to commemorate the town's approximately 1,500 murdered Jews, and I feel sad and empty as we drive away.

Our next stop is Kazanow, just a short drive, just over seventeen-kilometres from Skaryszew. My research has shown that my great-grandfather Szulima and some of his brothers came from Kazanow and my great-grandparents married there in 1880. Smaller than Skaryszew, the village is more appealing, with pretty rows of cottages across from the old Jewish cemetery. We park the car on the side of the road and look across to a lush field and a rather surreal scene. The original metal gate is still standing, held firmly on either side by a pair of small brick pillars, but the rest of the wall is gone on both sides: a gate protecting nothing.

Tomasz and I wander through the open field, where nothing remains of the headstones that once stood there. We get down on our hands and knees at times, using our bare hands to pull back the grass and pebbles, searching for any signs of gravestones or markers, but we find none. Tomasz asks a local resident if he knows what happened to the stones from the cemetery. The man shakes his head and tells us that local people took the last few remaining headstones many years ago and crushed them to make steps or paths. My heart sinks at such desecration; I want to cry.

We leave Kazanow in the early afternoon and drive just about fifty kilometers eastward towards Pulawy, where my grandfather Morris (Moshe Aron) and my father's grandfather, Lejb Goldman, lived. The landscape is changing from flat farmland to small, undulating, verdant hills topped with large tracts of rich, dark, forested land. I look out of the window at the beautiful countryside with mixed emotions. It is difficult to imagine all the brutality and the immense loss of life that occurred in such a picturesque place. I sleep for at least half of the journey; the pace of the trip and the time change from Canada are beginning to catch up with me.

As we approach Pulawy, traffic patterns begin to change and I wake up just as we cross the bridge over the Vistula River into the town. The river features several sandbars and lush riverbanks.

"How lovely," I say. "It looks like a perfect place for picnicking, or hiking and swimming."

"No, not so," says Tomasz. "That river is badly polluted — it is not a safe place to swim." It's strange how looks can be deceiving.

Pulawy is much larger than I imagined. During its tumultuous history, the town changed hands between Poland and Russia several times and also, I learned, changed names. I knew that my father's family came from a place called Novo Alexander. Although I found similar place names in Russia, I couldn't find such a town in Poland. Eventually I located a map from the 1800s; when I carefully lined up the latitude and longitude of Novo Alexander, I discovered that it was in the same location as Pulawy. So I researched the history of Pulawy and found that it had indeed been called Novo Alexander. Prior to World War I, however, the Russians lost control of the city during a battle and it reverted to the name Pulawy under Polish rule, where it has remained to this day.

Due to time constraints and the rain, we're unable to spend too much time in Pulawy, but we pass impressive former palaces and manicured parks that belonged to Polish royalty from a bygone era. The earliest known Jewish settlement dates back to 1572; larger groups put down roots in the second half of the eighteenth century when the community became a prominent political and intellectual hub. Confined to the Pulawy ghetto during World War II, the 3,600 Jewish residents were eventually deported by the Nazis to Sobibor, a death camp located on Poland's eastern boundary.

The rain begins again as we drive towards the historic spa town of Kazimierz Dolny, a short distance from Pulawy. Approaching the town, Tomasz pulls over and stops the car beside a wall made up of Jewish cemetery headstones with single stones standing in front of them. It is an imposing memorial to the people whose graves have suffered such indignity after being removed from the original cemeteries, but at least these markers were salvaged. I get out and take some photographs while trying to dodge the rain, but lightning chases me back to the car as thunder shakes the ground. Black clouds blot out the sky and the windshield wipers can barely keep up with the deluge as we drive on.

As we near the town, the sky brightens, and we drive past houses that look across the road to the Vistula River. We enter Kazimierz Dolny, once the summer home of Polish royalty, and park the car near the picturesque square. Tomasz tells me that the town was also home to many Jews. The royal family welcomed the Jewish community by offering incentives for them to build their homes and set up businesses. We walk around the market square with its unique buildings, some quite large and constructed of wood, with a Russian influence and curving rooflines. A small, ancient wooden structure is in the process of being renovated, and unfortunately it is impossible to go inside: this is the original old synagogue, which would have been the first building the Jews built here to attract others to the community.

It begins to drizzle again and Tomasz and I decide to eat our evening meal in the town before heading on to Lublin. We choose an old "Jewish style" restaurant. We sit at a table in a very dark room with rough wood floors and wooden tables and chairs stained dark brown. On each table, two glowing candlesticks are placed close to the windows, reminding us of Shabbat (Sabbath) except it is Tuesday. The menu features all the Jewish comfort foods that I was brought up on: chicken soup, *knaidlach* (matzoh balls), kreplach (dumplings), brisket, *cholent* (stew), and chopped liver. Anticipating a great meal, I order chopped liver to start and *cholent* for the main course.

The chopped liver arrives and the texture and taste is nothing like I have ever had before; it doesn't look or taste like chopped liver and after only two bites I gently push the plate to one side. I cut into the brisket that is mixed in with the *cholent*; the meat is tougher than leather, and I also put it to one side while I eat the beans and lentils. I know I'm going to be hungry later, and I make a conscious decision to go back to basics when choosing food at the next restaurant. After paying the bill, Tomasz and I walk back to the car. The sun has set and the sky is darkening as we drive towards Lublin, our final stop of the day.

By the time we reach Lublin, the sky is pitch-black. Tomasz pulls up in front of the hotel just as the heavens open up, and our umbrellas do little to protect us from the blowing wind and driving rain as we grab our bags and run into the hotel. The staff is friendly and the hotel seems pleasant, if a little austere. When I get to my room I flop down on the bed and the duvet almost wraps itself around me. I'm dog-tired and my head is swimming. The room has exceptionally high ceilings and there seems to be marble everywhere — I later discover that a bank occupied the building prior to being turned into a hotel. Opening the heavy drapes, I look out the window at the rain. A streetcar goes by, perhaps the last one of the night. The streets appear to be empty. Yet even in the darkness I feel a sense of belonging that I have not felt in any of the other Polish cities or towns I have visited. After a warm bath, I climb under the fluffy duvet, turn off the lights and sleep through the night.

§

My alarm clock wakes me early. I shower and feel refreshed. The sky has cleared and the sun shines brightly as Tomasz and I walk towards the Lublin Castle and old Jewish quarter. The architecture is very different from that of Kraków and the buildings remind me of the Russian influence of another era.

Tomasz begins telling me the history of Jewish Lublin as we walk toward the old city. He tells me that Lublin is one of the oldest cities in Eastern Poland and was once was home to one of the largest Jewish communities that enjoyed self-rule. Jewish Lublin flourished for several hundred years as a centre of education and knowledge and included renowned yeshivas and publishers of religious books. Many Hasidic spiritual leaders came from Lublin. It was also the birth place of prominent writers, including brothers Israel Joshua and Isaac Bashevis Singer. I remember my mother telling me that my grandfather loved going to the Jewish theatre in Lublin, and that many of the plays were performed in Yiddish.

Finally, Tomasz explains that when the Nazis seized Poland in 1939, the Jewish population of Lublin and the nearby towns and villages totalled in the hundreds of thousands. By the end of World War II, only a handful of Jews from the region had survived the Holocaust. Today, there are very few Jews living in Lublin.

We walk to the colourful market near in the old town, where the old Jewish ritual slaughterhouse still stands behind the covered stalls. Elderly Polish women sell fruit, vegetables and flowers while shoppers bargain with animated sellers. We then walk toward the Grodzka Gate, erected as it stands now in 1787. Behind the gate, in the direction of the castle, stretches another world once full of Jewish homes, in which the Shabbat candles could be seen burning on Friday evenings. This area was often referred to as the "Jerusalem of Poland." We look down at the open spaces surrounding the castle, trying to imagine the intricate network of streets with tightly packed houses that once filled the area before the Nazis destroyed them. Almost all of Lublin's Jews spoke Yiddish, and unlike in Kraków, many of them did not speak Polish.

As we pass through the Grodzka Gate, I experience a feeling of comfort and familiarity, as though I've been here before. I look down the street and point out a building in the distance to Tomasz, guessing that it may have been a theatre; as we get closer we can read an old sign on the boarded-up building, and sure enough, it was the old Jewish theatre. Around the town square many of the buildings featuring colourful painted facades are being restored to their former splendour. Not far away we spot a Jewish style restaurant and the former Jewish orphanage.

We make our way to the old Jewish cemetery, one of Jewish Lublin's great historical monuments. It is locked and Tomasz leaves me briefly while he goes in search of the key. He returns a short while later and unlocks the gate, and we begin our tour. The cemetery functioned from 1541 to 1829 and is one of the oldest and most precious Jewish necropolises in Poland. Despite the fact it has been recognized as a historical monument for over a century, the cemetery has been vandalized several times. It experienced extreme neglect during Poland's Communist era, but during the 1980s the Society for the Care of Jewish Cultural Monuments in Lublin tidied and catalogued the cemetery. However, between 1988 and 1991 vandals destroyed forty of the eighty remaining gravestones.

We walk around the monuments while the ground rises steeply and quickly, some historians believe the cemetery contains several layers of headstones.

A concrete path takes us from one important *matzevah*, or monument, to another. Some monuments date as far back as the late 1500s.

Further along is the enclosed tomb of Yakov Yitzhak Ha-Levi Horowitz, a Polish Hasid known as "the Seer" of Lublin. Tomasz explains that Horowitz became well known for his psychic powers and that he focused his teachings on morality. Horowitz is said to have walked around with his eyes covered by a blindfold to prevent him from seeing what he believed to be an immoral world.

Others buried in the Old Jewish cemetery include Shalom ben Yosef Shachna, Shlomo ben Yechiel Luria, known as the Maharshal, and Moshe Montalto. We lock the gates, return the key and make our way to the new Jewish cemetery. Established in 1829, it is the final resting place of over 50,000 people, including members of the dynasty of *tzaddik* Jacob Leib Eiger. The restored shrine of Meir Shapiro can also be found here although it is only of symbolic importance as his remains were transferred to a cemetery in Jerusalem in 1958.

We walk back to the car and take a short drive to the Lublin Academy of Sages (Yeshivit Chachmei Lublin), which turns out to be the highlight of Lublin for me.

As we walk onto the grounds, Tomasz explains that the yeshiva was established in 1930 by Yehuda Meir Shapiro, a brilliant man who devoted his life to the study of the Talmud. Shapiro also wrote several highly acclaimed books. He was not only respected within the orthodox community; he was also elected as a member of the Polish parliament. When he died, his funeral was attended by hundreds of pious Jews along with members of the Polish government.

The large building is an imposing five floors, not including the lower level. The yeshiva operated for only nine years before the beginning of World War II. Scholars came from all over the world to study, and the school was renowned not only for its rigorous curriculum but also for the high calibre of graduating students. Some successful graduates went to the United States and took up rabbinical posts upon completion of their studies.

The Nazis took over the building when they captured Lublin during World War II. Most of the contents were removed and destroyed. The building was eventually returned to the Jewish community by the Polish government; however, the building was in disrepair after being used as a medical school. It now relies on donations from Jewish communities from around the world for the money to complete much-needed renovations and perform continual maintenance.

The main entrance of the building is open and as we walk towards the doors, Tomasz stops and speaks with a man pruning bushes. The building is surrounded by gardens planted with thousands of trees. The man looks at me while talking with Tomasz, and his face breaks into a huge smile. He beckons us to follow him into the building. We walk into the newly renovated main sanctuary and then into a smaller one beside it. Both have been returned to their former simplicity. Large windows that had been bricked in under Communism have been repaired, and the main sanctuary is now full of light. We walk up the beautiful, wide, original staircase, and the gardener leads us out to the balcony overlooking the grounds at the front. I suddenly feel quite humbled knowing that I am standing where great Jewish intellects, in particular Yehuda Meir Shapiro, stood as they acknowledged enthusiastic students below.

We then walk all the way down to the basement where considerable work is underway repairing the original *mikvah*. Because walls were blocked off during the Communist years, no one knew if the ritual baths still existed. With the guidance of the original building plans, Jewish officials removed the cinder bricks with much celebration when they discovered the original *mikvah* still intact.

The gardener takes obvious pride in showing us around and refuses to take any money for his efforts; however, I purchase a small booklet and postcard and leave a donation for the yeshiva. While it is unlikely that the building will ever function again as an academy of Jewish learning, it will serve as a place for Jews to visit now and in the future. There are also plans for the first European Museum of Hasidism to be located in the building. The postcard that I purchase is a photograph from the official re-opening of the building in 2007. It shows a large number of guests from around the world celebrating the occasion on February 9, which happens to be my birthday.

One of the purposes of my visit to Lublin is to research the Goldman and Edelstein families. A pious Orthodox Jew, my grandfather changed his family name from Goldman to Gold when he immigrated to England, but my father was originally a Goldman, and my grandfather Morris (Moshe Aron) an Edelstein (originally Ajdelsztajn). I have uncovered information as far back as my great-grandfather Lejb Goldman's generation, but no farther. Research is particularly difficult because Goldman was a very common name in Jewish Poland, equivalent to Smith in the English language. Also, both of these families intermarried several times, and Lejb married more than once, so the genealogical search for the Goldman family remains a work in progress.

Tomasz and I go to the regional archives and begin reading through dozens of books filled with birth, marriage and death registrations mostly written in Russian. Each record is a handwritten summary of the event, approximately half a page. Tomasz speaks and reads Russian, but since our time is at a premium, we leave the research in the capable hands of the Lublin archives.

§

We skip lunch and drive to Majdanek, in the suburbs of Lublin. The sky is filled with black clouds and various shades of grey, and it is cool and windy. This is the first concentration camp that I have ever visited, and it is a sobering experience. I know that at least one of my relatives, Benjamin's older brother Yosef Albaum, died in the camp. Established in 1941 by Heinrich Himmler, Majdanek is where the Nazis murdered the majority of the Jewish population of Lublin and the surrounding areas.

The grounds look enormous. As we enter through the gates, I notice that suburban Lublin homes back onto the camp fields and wonder how the residents of these houses feel, knowing what occurred in the camp. I feel cold as we walk along the road.

Tomasz tells me that the camp sits on well over 600 acres of land and, at one time, contained several hundred buildings that held thousands of prisoners. Few of the original buildings remain. The camp initially held Soviet prisoners of war who were used as slave labour. Later, thousands of Jews were used as slave labourers, and those who became ill were murdered in the gas chambers of Majdanek along with deported Jewish victims of the Holocaust.

Majdanek was one of the first camps to be liberated toward the end of the war, and as Soviet forces approached in July 1944, the Nazis hastily tried to erase as much evidence of mass murder as possible. But the army arrived sooner than anticipated and the Nazis fled, unable to cover up all their crimes against humanity. When the Soviets entered the camp, they found thousands of prisoners of war and substantial proof of the murders that had taken place in the camp. The gas chamber still stands today, along with the crematoria that the Nazis only partially destroyed before fleeing. Since I visited Majdanek in 2007, the museum has reconstructed some of the barracks, which are now used for display purposes.

We walk towards the massive monument, in the form of a mausoleum, built over the remains of the ashes of thousands of murdered Jews. The wind blows around us as we stand at the immense raised concrete structure. Looking across a field, I see a large carved marble stone commemorating the 18,000 Jews of Lublin who died as the result of a mass execution undertaken by the SS. Naming it with ironic cruelty Aktion Erntefest, or Operation Harvest Festival, the Nazis planned to exterminate the remaining Jews in the Lublin District, the Lublin Ghetto and an area of Poland that was annexed by the Germans and known as the General Government.

Tomasz explains that the Nazis prepared for the operation at Majdanek by assigning hundreds of prisoners to dig three large trenches — I can see these trenches as I look across the field near the mausoleum. Then on November 3, 1943, guards led more than 18,000 prisoners from the buildings in the camp and from trucks, forced them to strip and then marched them to the trenches. The naked prisoners were then forced to lie in the trenches and were systematically shot. According to the United States Holocaust Museum, music was blared over the camp's loudspeakers in an effort to drown out the sounds of murder taking place. In total, approximately 42,000 Jews died during Aktion Erntefest.

I light a memorial candle that I've brought with me in memory of Yosef Albaum. The cold wind is gusting and it takes several attempts to keep it burning. I quietly recite a prayer in his memory and for all the victims murdered in Majdanek during the Holocaust. I turn and look at the ashes under the structure, which mysteriously do not blow about in the wind. I am angry and inconsolable; my eyes well up with tears that sting as they roll down my cheeks, and the cold wind whips around my face.

We walk towards the showers, gas chamber and crematoria, and I cannot remember feeling so cold in May. Rose bushes planted outside the buildings are a reminder of the psychological games that the Nazis played on their victims. How can a building surrounded by beautiful flowers house such immoral acts? I walk into a concrete room with blue stains on the walls from Zyklon B, the deadly gas dropped through small doors in the roof after the SS tightly packed the gas chamber with their victims. A wave of claustrophobia comes over me and I have to walk outside. I walk into a crematorium, where there are still ashes in the open doors. Tomasz takes a step back without speaking, allowing me the emotional space to absorb the horrors before my eyes. To speak almost seems sacrilegious. As we leave the grounds I briefly stop and look back on the killing fields of the Nazi war machine of Majdanek, which took the lives of at least 60,000 innocent lives, mostly Jewish.

I leave Lublin with a mix of emotions. For all the joy I felt walking along the streets of the Jewish quarter, I feel equal sadness at the evil history that I have just seen in Majdanek. We begin our long drive back to Kraków in silence. The sky is still grey and dusk is approaching. Somewhere along the way I fall asleep.

I awaken to darkness as we approach Kraków from a district developed by the Communist government after the war. Full of high-rise apartment buildings that can only be described as ugly, the government built these huge grey boxes for function only. In some cases, crude attempts to brighten the appearance of the structures have been made by painting the exteriors in vivid colours, but little can be done to improve the architectural banality.

When Tomasz drops me off at my hotel, I am exhausted. I check in by email with my daughter in Toronto and send a quick message to my father. My mother is still resting comfortably in the hospital. The following day will be my last touring in Poland. We are driving west to Oświęcim and the mass Nazi extermination camp of Auschwitz. I fall asleep, my head swimming with reflections of what I have seen during the past two days and speculation of what is yet to come.

CHAPTER 7

My alarm jolts me from a deep sleep. I peel the duvet off and reluctantly shower, dress and make my way to the hotel dining room, where I hurry through breakfast. Tomasz is waiting for me outside the hotel. The drive from Kraków to Oświęcim is approximately sixty-eight kilometres. We make our way slowly through Kraków's morning rush hour, with the added hindrance of having to avoid erratic streetcars and the passengers who freely jump on and off them. I compliment Tomasz on his driving. We eventually leave the city behind for peaceful, lush farmland and small villages. Tomasz shares more history of the Polish Jews with me while we drive, but my mind is filled with uncertainty as to what we are about to see.

We cross the Sola River and negotiate a roundabout, but the approach to the town reveals no road signs indicating Auschwitz, only Oświęcim. We pass the massive I.G Farber factory where thousands of Jewish slave labourers worked; their only remuneration was the privilege of possibly surviving another day. It occurs to me that Benjamin may have been a slave labourer in Auschwitz during the ten months of incarceration before his death, but I have found no records that mention where he worked. I'm surprised to see remnants of wooden structures in subcamps, where labourers slept, and guard lookouts still stand near the factory; none of the buildings are properly preserved and they lack signage. We drive a short distance beside the river and make a right turn that brings us to the main entrance of Auschwitz. I look back and realize how close we are to the town.

Tomasz parks the car in one of the large parking lots and we walk towards the main building, where several tour groups of visitors have gathered inside the main entrance. They are speaking German, Italian, French, Korean, Japanese, Polish, Russian and English while waiting for their individual tour leaders. Tomasz is a certified Auschwitz guide, and he's allowed to take me independently through Auschwitz and nearby Birkenau.

Prior to my trip to Poland, Tomasz and I discussed the purpose of my visit in great detail, which includes tracing family members missing in the Holocaust. He contacted the archives at Auschwitz before I arrived regarding my search for details of Benjamin's death and made arrangements for me to meet privately with one of the archivists in the museum. We leave the main entrance and are ushered into a simply-furnished room, where we're joined by a sombre tall man in a suit and wearing glasses. He politely introduces himself and we shake hands. He is holding some photocopied papers and tells me they've found information regarding Benjamin Albaum.

I sit down and carefully read the documents in disbelief. I feel numb. Benjamin's death was recorded in 1943 at Auschwitz. Here it is, finally, the end of his life. No name, just his serial number, along with a handwritten list of other deaths on the same date. No information is given as to the cause of death.

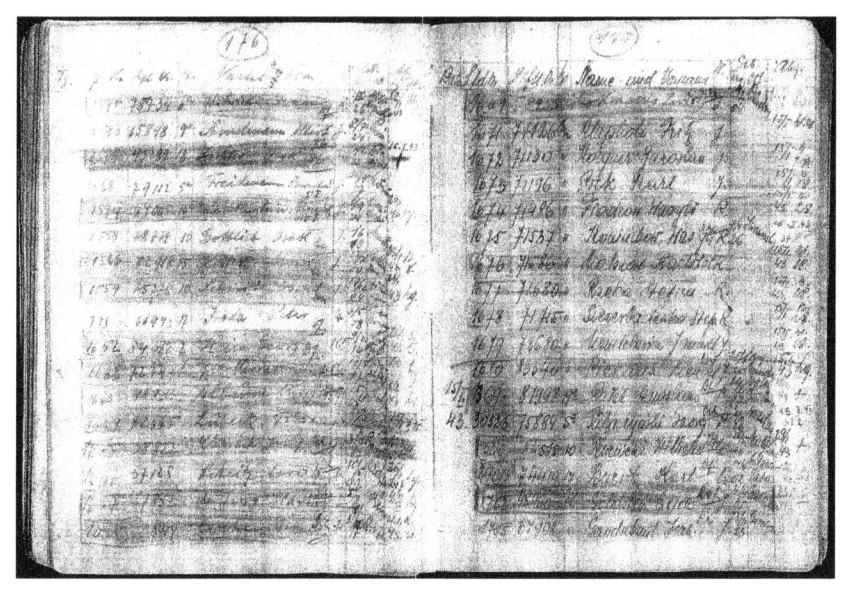

Handwritten record of Benjamin's death with his prisoner name and number. Sent to me by the Auschwitz-Birkenau State Museum after my visit in 2007. In the original, entries are shaded in what appears to be coloured pencil (red, greenish-blue, orange). I'm still trying to establish the reason for the different colours.

A Stone for Benjamin

I know that the Nazis destroyed 90 percent of the documents in the camp, so to have this written confirmation is unusual. We sit quietly for a few minutes and I thank the archivist for his efforts. He seems genuinely sorry to be the bearer of such sad news. He asks me for my address since he is not allowed to hand me copies of records directly. He says that an official, stamped and certified photocopy of the documents will be mailed to my home during the next few days. It is difficult to express my feelings as he shakes hands with Tomasz and me; I thank him again, yet what am I thanking him for?

Benjamin's death record (prisoner number 48883, third column from the left, first entry). Sent to me by the Auschwitz-Birkenau State Museum after my visit in 2007.

I feel an urgent need to see the rest of this place of mass murder and evil. Auschwitz comprises three prime camps: Auschwitz I, the main camp; Auschwitz II, or Birkenau, the extermination camp; and Auschwitz III, or Monowitz, a work camp. As well there are numerous subcamps. Tomasz and I walk toward the main courtyard into Auschwitz 1, which seems smaller than I anticipated. I look up and see the famous metal sign, *"Arbeit Macht Frei"* ("work makes you free"), above the gates. We walk toward some of the brick buildings that housed the prisoners who, like Benjamin, became slave labourers until they died from disease and hunger or miraculously survived. We walk past the barbed-wire fence and guard post that separated the men from women. The Nazis electrified the fences, and inmates sometimes committed suicide by throwing themselves on the barbed wire. But the Nazis made a major error when wiring the camp, and the horrific nighttime suicides threw the entire camp into total darkness. None of the huge searchlights installed in guard towers would work following a suicide, an oversight that enabled some prisoners to escape.

The barracks at Auschwitz, with barbed wire that was once electrified.
I took this photo during my 2007 trip.

We continue walking towards Block 20, where France has an exhibition of photographs and documents concerning some of the men, women and children that France deported and the Nazis murdered in Auschwitz. I look at the photographs and walk around the building feeling chilled. According to camp records, Benjamin died in Block 20, the contagious diseases ward. The Nazis conducted experiments on prisoners with typhus, typhoid fever, tuberculosis and other infectious diseases in this building. SS doctors administered untried drugs provided by various pharmaceutical companies, including Bayer — not to help the patients but to observe the effects of the medications. Many victims suffered from severe and painful reactions, and ultimately most prisoners in the ward died from the drug trials or the disease. Prisoners rarely left the infirmary alive, and if they did survive, SS doctors frequently murdered their prey with a lethal injection of phenol.

I can only speculate as to what the Nazis did to Benjamin during his ten months of incarceration at the camp. My mind races again. Joseph Mengele, the renowned "Angel of Death," arrived in Auschwitz in May 1943, the same month that Benjamin died. Did Mengele murder Benjamin? I keep looking back at Block 20, too consumed with anger and contempt to cry. There is no real conversation between Tomasz and me; there is only his commentary as we make our way through the various barracks with different exhibitions, some more shocking than others.

Photographing certain exhibits is forbidden in Auschwitz, and Tomasz firmly tells some visitors to stop when they try to take pictures of prisoners' personal belongings. The exhibits of human hair, shoes and glasses are particularly difficult to view, as are the tight rows of wooden bunks where prisoners slept squeezed together without adequate bedding and next to no heat. I am unprepared, though, for how upsetting I find the latrine.

Located in the men's section of Auschwitz I, the latrine was shared by all the prisoners. The toilets consist of extremely long wooden benches in two rows back to back. Numerous circular openings are cut into the seats, with very little space between each hole. Below is a trough to collect the human waste; the Nazis assigned prisoners to clean out the latrine with buckets. I walk through the building slowly, imagining the unbearable stench and feeling the indignity that prisoners must have suffered, forced to relieve themselves in full view of one other. All I can think about is Benjamin, subjected to long hours of harsh labour, beatings, starvation, disease and finally the humiliation of using the latrine. I have to leave the enclosure; I feel dizzy.

We enter Block 11, where the Nazis tortured prisoners and tested the deadly gas Zyklon B in the basement. Finally, we enter the building where SS officers tried prisoners before a kangaroo court for stealing a piece of bread or some other minor infraction. Always found guilty, the prisoners would be forced to strip and escorted outside to a back wall in the courtyard where they were shot. Blocked-off windows in the buildings beside the quadrangle prevented other prisoners from seeing and hearing the murders taking place.

As we wander from building to building, Tomasz explains the mechanics of the operation of the camp and the Nazi regime. I greatly admire his knowledge and sensitivity in allowing me time to process information, and he gives me the utmost respect by stepping back and allowing me my mental and physical space when I view the most difficult exhibits.

We are ready to visit Birkenau, which sits about two and a half kilometres from Auschwitz. Tomasz gives me some background information about Birkenau and tells me that the camp was built in 1941 on the site of the small village of Brzezinka, a short distance from Auschwitz. The Nazis originally intended the camp to be used to imprison captured Russian prisoners of war but they also used it as a camp for Gypsies, families and women. Stockpiled stolen possessions from murdered Jews were also kept in Birkenau. Ultimately, it became primarily a death camp. The Nazis turned Birkenau into a mass killing machine beyond one's imagination, murdering hundreds of thousands of Jews, sometimes through the night, before the camp was liberated in 1945.

We walk toward the railway tracks and the unloading area where the convoys, each carrying approximately one thousand Jews, arrived — often several in one day. Operated by an engineer from the originating country in Europe, the train stopped at the gates of Auschwitz where its operator disembarked. A Nazi would take over, slowly moving the train past the gates so that the driver never saw the inside of the camp. That said, engineers must have wondered what happened to the thousands of Jews they brought to the camp.

After the train arrived, the SS unlocked each cattle car and soldiers with menacing dogs would begin yelling at the prisoners, telling them to get out of the train. Guards ordered the new arrivals to leave their luggage on the platform, telling them that it would be delivered later. Whether selected for slave labour or the gas chambers, victims never received their belongings. Instead, other prisoners gathered together the bags and took them to the brick building nicknamed "Kanada" by inmates; since Canada symbolized freedom, it was the place where they all wanted to go. Workers sorted precious metals and money along with clothing; all were sent back to Germany to either be melted down or reused. But not by Jews — there were none left.

Close by on the rails is an exhibit of a single cattle car. It is much smaller than I had imagined, and I find it difficult to envision fifty to a hundred people jammed inside each car for days on end with luggage, nowhere to sit, no light, no fresh air, no food or water and just one bucket in which to relieve themselves. I cannot bring myself to look inside. A gust of wind springs up with a few drops of rain, and I do not attempt to protect myself; the moisture on my head and face feels cleansing, as though it is washing away the evil that has made me feel literally dirty.

I need some time alone with my thoughts and I decide to walk beside the railway tracks while Tomasz moves the car from Auschwitz to Birkenau. I purposely take that route. I want to get a sense of what arriving prisoners saw, since most of them walked from the selection lines towards the gas chambers. When I look back to the buildings in Auschwitz, the two camps seem closer together than they first appear. I pass the skeletons of wooden huts that once held prisoners. The huts had no heat, just another method the Nazis used to slowly kill the prisoners if dysentery or typhus did not come first.

The sun is peeking through the clouds and the rain has stopped. I hold my head high, and as I get closer to the end of the railway line at Birkenau I recall Eichmann's list of eleven million Jews that he prepared for the "final solution." I walk tall, almost defiantly, thinking, "You didn't get us all." At the end of the line I see several memorial candles on the metal rails, some flickering and some burned out. I manage to light my own candle in spite of the wind and I leave it on the rail. I step back and quietly repeat a prayer for the dead; I cannot stop my tears.

I walk over to the metal plaques on the ground and look at the inscriptions in various languages, including English, commemorating the murders at Auschwitz. They read:

> Forever let this place be a cry of despair and a warning to humanity where the Nazis murdered about one and a half million men, women and children, mainly Jews from various countries of Europe. Auschwitz-Birkenau 1940–1945.

The areas surrounding the grounds are luxuriant, green and peaceful. I hear cuckoos calling from the weeping willows. This bucolic place also served as a holding area where the Nazis would place their waiting prey when the gassings could not keep pace with the constant arrival of trainloads of prisoners. Psychology played a huge role in controlling the unsuspecting victims. After spending days locked in cattle cars, the innocent captives welcomed rest in this serene spot.

Tomasz meets up with me and we walk in silence. Some Polish school children, probably no more than thirteen years old, are running and laughing along the train tracks. I'm disappointed in their disrespect but choose not to say anything as I look questioningly at their chaperone.

We walk past the reconstructed wooden gallows erected for the public hanging of Rudolf Franz Ferdinand Höss, the first commandant of Auschwitz. Responsible for the expansion of the camp, Höss also created the mass killing machine that it became.

Transferred to Polish authorities after being convicted at a military tribunal in Nuremberg in 1946, Höss was found guilty by the Supreme National Tribunal of murdering three and a half million people and sentenced to death by hanging. Even though I don't believe in capital punishment, I find it difficult to rationalize why he did not have to experience the slow death of asphyxiation that his victims endured in the gas chambers.

During the final weeks of the war, the Nazis, knowing they were almost defeated, destroyed all the gas chambers in Auschwitz and Birkenau as the Russians closed in on the camp. I decide not to enter one of the smaller chambers, reconstructed in Auschwitz I after the war. I saw the interior of the gas chamber in Majdanek, including the blue stains on the walls from the Zyklon B. I try to envisage how victims felt as guards forced more naked people into the concrete chamber. Jammed in, they watched as the doors were sealed shut and had no space to move because the gas worked better with heat: the more bodies in the chamber, the faster the victims died. I then picture my own family during the fifteen to twenty minutes it took for them to suffocate. Pessa, Sara, Frida and Roland Albaum all perished in those gas chambers. Somehow public hanging seems too easy a death for Rudolf Höss.

I am mentally drained, physically tired and ready to leave Auschwitz. I stop at the store and purchase some books to take home with me before Tomasz and I walk to the car.

It is early afternoon and we haven't eaten since breakfast. I'm not sure if I'm hungry, but we stop at a restaurant that seems very close to the camp grounds. I order a salad but find it difficult to eat or even stay in the restaurant, watching others as they consume their food, animated in conversation. I feel guilty for eating, for sitting at a table with a white tablecloth and for being served food, even just for talking. I finish my meal quickly, pay the bill and leave.

There are times when silence is best. Tomasz and I hardly speak as we drive back to Kraków. What I have learned this day has left an indelible mark on me. What I have seen is tangible proof that humans are capable of absolute evil.

It is still light when we arrive back at my hotel in Kraków, and I go to my room. I feel dirty, anxious to wash away my thoughts, but cannot decide if I should rest or take a shower. I try lying down on the bed and close my eyes, but all I can see are visions of Nazis with dogs beating prisoners. I decide to go for a walk. The hotel is located near the large market square in Kraków. I think about having a coffee in one of the restaurants that dot the perimeter, but discomfort and guilt wash over me again as they did earlier in the restaurant near Auschwitz, and I quickly head back to the hotel. I check my BlackBerry and exchange emails with my family in Toronto and London. My mother is still in the hospital and looking forward to my homecoming in a few days, and right now all I really want is to hug her and hold her in my arms.

I pack my bags in preparation for my departure the following morning. I would like to leave Kraków tonight; the events of the day consume me and I cannot think of anything else. I can't eat and I turn on the television as a distraction. Emotionally exhausted, I climb under the duvet and toss and turn. I close my eyes, but all I can see are the faces of Nazis. I get up and check the locks on my door and turn the light on in the bathroom; I feel like a child but I am not going to be able to sleep in total darkness. I lie in bed, anxious to leave, and watch the sun rise. During the drive to the airport, I thank Tomasz for his research, planning and guidance, without which I could never have undertaken this trip. We promise to stay in touch. My flight departs on time, and as we soar into the cloudy sky over Kraków, I don't look back. All I can think about is my mother waiting for me to come home. I want to hold her frail body, see her smile and look into her eyes while I describe my journey and show her pictures of these places where our roots run deep. I know there is much more to learn about Jewish Poland and my own roots there, and despite my painful memories of the extermination camps of Majdanek and Auschwitz, I know I will return some day.

As for France, I have compartmentalized my feelings about it: on one side, love of the country and culture; on the other, French complicity in the deportation of so many Jews. To integrate them into a whole is too difficult for me.

After spending a few days with family in England, I return to Toronto. I go directly from the airport to the hospital to see my mother, who with great effort holds her thin arms open wide. I gently wrap my arms around her, neither one of us wanting to let go. She seems so fragile, yet her beautiful deep blue eyes — as I now know, the same colour as Benjamin's — glisten as I describe my journey and show her my photographs. Doctors tell me they can do little more, and my father and I bring her home by ambulance within a few days. My mother is weak and gradually begins to refuse food. She returns to the hospital at the beginning of June. I take my father each day to visit and he sits beside her for hours, their frail hands entwined. Before I take him home each day, my father kisses my mother. The two of them look deeply into each other's eyes and whisper, "I love you." On June 11, 2012, my mother slips away.

My parents spent almost sixty-five years devoted to each other and I worry how my father will cope without my mother. My father suffers from Parkinson's along with serious kidney problems. My mother, acutely aware of his ill health, made me promise before she died that I would look after him. This is an easy promise for me to make: my father and I have a special bond and it is not difficult for me to care for him. After choosing not to go on dialysis, his health quickly declines. My father passes away ten months after my mother though I know our bond will stay with me for the rest of my life.

After my father's death I need time to recoup. Though he has told me I must write this book, I'm worn out after months of caring for both of my parents, and I opt to give myself a break from writing so that I can recharge my batteries. It doesn't matter how old you are when you lose your parents, it takes time to adjust to the loss. I still miss both of them. I particularly miss the animated political discussions I would have with my father when I dropped by their house at the end of the day. And I miss my mother reminding me to button up my coat in bitterly cold weather. I spent almost three years caring for both of my parents while working, but I have no regrets; I would not hesitate to do it again.

CHAPTER 8

During the summer of 2010, my husband and I visit Paris together for a few days. We take the metro everywhere and walk for miles along the Left Bank. This is the Paris that I know and love. We decide to visit the Shoah Memorial and as we walk through a small park on our way to the metro, I stop and pick up a stone from a flower bed.

Once through the doors at the memorial, we walk over to the wall of names and find Benjamin, along with Pessa, Frida, Roland and other members of the Albaum family who perished in the Holocaust. We light the memorial candle that I brought with me and leave it, along with the little stone, on the floor in front of the wall where Benjamin's name is engraved. I say a prayer in silence.

My husband has not seen the rest of the memorial and we explore exhibits inside the building. Finally we go down the stairs to see the eternal flame and the ashes from the Nazi extermination camps. After spending time in the bookstore, we make our way back to the wall of names. I trace my finger over Benjamin's name one more time. I feel a certain amount of comfort each time I visit the memorial, knowing that Benjamin and his family have been remembered.

Taking my hand, my husband leads me across the courtyard where we exit the Shoah Memorial to walk down a quaint street. We are in the fourth arrondissement, in the Marais, just south of where Benjamin lived and where Jews have resided since the thirteenth century. The cobbled streets and tall old buildings have made the area popular with Parisians and tourists. The Marais still has a good-sized Jewish population, and rue des Rosiers and its neighbouring streets contain Jewish restaurants, bakeries and delis along with bookstores and synagogues.

The sun is shining and we walk across a narrow street toward a charming café. It is warm and we sit outside. We order our food and I watch the family beside us in animated conversation with their young children, who are eating, laughing and playing with their small dog. My mind drifts to Benjamin and I wonder if he ever got to share the simple, carefree pleasure of eating outside at a café with Pessa and their three children, without wearing his identifying yellow star.

CHAPTER 9

My search for Benjamin seems incomplete without a visit to Israel, in particular to Yad Vashem, where I began my search for him, and where the record of his death will be forever preserved. My husband is invited to speak in Israel at the beginning of July 2012 and I accompany him on the trip.

We spend the first nine days in Jerusalem and then take a tour of the country. The Old City of Jerusalem, the newly developing Israel and the Israeli people are intoxicating. This is my first visit and I cannot get enough of the history. I walk to the Old City several times, going through the Arab, Armenian, Christian and Jewish quarters. We visit the Kotel (the Western or Wailing Wall) on our first day. I begin walking toward the wall and pause for a moment, realizing the solemnity of where I am standing. No one is speaking; they are only praying in silence. White, black, Jew or non-Jew, we are all equal at the foot of the wall. I make my approach and kiss my hand before I touch this amazing piece of history. I pray for our children and grandchildren and for peace in Israel and around the world. Before I leave, I place a handwritten message in a crack between two stones, asking that our children be granted long, peaceful and happy lives.

I visit Yad Vashem twice; I am alone during the first visit and with my husband and our tour group the second time. Touring the museum prompts memories of my trips to Auschwitz and Majdanek, but these are not places one ever forgets. Then I enter the Hall of Names. Over two million Pages of Testimony are housed in the circular hall with its high, domed roof; short biographies of each Holocaust victim have been submitted by family, friends or acquaintances and are stored there in black cases stacked high and neatly against the walls. The curved ceiling is ten meters high, and the interior surface is covered with approximately six hundred photographs, along with fragments from the Pages of Testimony.

I find myself looking up. The height and size of the dome makes the number of pictures seem larger. There are faces of children and adults, some smiling and some serious. I stand there for several minutes studying the photographs; six hundred faces represent just a fraction of the six million Jewish victims of the Holocaust. Yet, in stark contrast to the final moments of their lives, there is serenity and peace in the Hall.

I wander into the computer room and speak with one of the staff. Only two of us are in the room yet I find myself whispering. I want to register the members of my family murdered in the Holocaust. I have twenty-three forms to complete, including one with additional information for Benjamin, and I realize that it will take a considerable amount of time to fill in each page. I speak to a soft-spoken, gentle man who works in the room. He encourages me to take the forms with me to complete in Canada, and then to return them to Yad Vashem with photographs attached to relevant pages of my testimony.

I walk back through the circular hall and along the hallway to the large glass doors that lead out of the building. I step outside onto a balcony, and the magnificent panorama takes my breath away. Yad Vashem is located high in a forest near Mount Herzl; I gaze at the peaceful valley below, absorbing a view that is in stark contrast to the recollections of evil I've just seen in the museum. Lush green trees stand out against the vivid blue sky, and a gentle breeze rustles their leaves. I am hesitant to leave, but after a few minutes I take the tranquil path that leads to the Hall of Remembrance.

The building is a daunting single-story structure with two large iron doors and no windows. It is almost completely dark inside except for the Eternal Flame, which burns continuously beside a tomb containing ashes of victims from twenty-two of the most notorious extermination camps in Europe. I stand at the far end and read the names of the camps, and I am overcome with sadness knowing how many of my family were murdered or died in some of these places. I also think about all the victims whose fate I don't know, including cousins and my grandmothers' sisters, who disappeared without a trace. Their last known address is in the Radom ghetto. The Nazis murdered most of the residents either in the ghetto or in the death camp of Treblinka, though some died in Majdanek and Auschwitz. Others were forced into trucks, driven to remote areas outside of Radom and shot.

My husband and I stand together in silence, absorbing the solemnity of the building and the moment. Then he takes my hand and we make our way towards the doors. As we walk outside into the burning sunshine, I wipe the tears from my eyes.

The swings of emotions are enormous at Yad Vashem. Upon exiting a darkened, sombre room, a visitor walks along peaceful pathways in vivid sunshine surrounded by large trees that sway gently in the warm breeze. We make our way down the Avenue of the Righteous Among the Nations, a path honouring thousands of non-Jews who selflessly risked their own lives to save many Jews during the Holocaust.

It is the Children's Memorial that has the greatest emotional impact on me. The memorial is a tribute to the one and a half million Jewish children murdered in the Holocaust. The building has been created in a cavern that sits partially underground. No one speaks as we walk towards the entrance. We move through the dark room single file, holding a handrail, and all I can see in the blackness are thousands of flickering candles overhead, around me and below my feet. I listen to the names of the murdered children being read aloud as I continue to walk through the room. I feel as if I'm walking through the Milky Way and every flicker of light is a lost child. I remember Benjamin's children, Sara, Frida and Roland, especially how Frida and Roland were separated from their mother by the French police and sent on their own among strangers to Auschwitz. My husband walks behind me with his hand on my shoulder. We are unable to speak when we emerge from the darkened space.

Making our way to the main entrance, we meet up with the rest of our tour. We are a diverse group of people of different nationalities with various ethnic and religious backgrounds. Yad Vashem has affected us all deeply and the mood is serious and quiet as we return to Jerusalem.

The balance of our tour takes us to the many highlights in Israel and the West Bank, including centuries-old synagogues, mosques and churches. We visit the Kotel again, tour the exterior of the Dome of the Rock, a shrine on the Temple Mount in the Old City, and listen to the hypnotic and haunting Muslim call to prayer that occurs each evening in Jerusalem. We browse in shops and eat in restaurants where Palestinians and Israelis eat side by side, and we wend our way through the Arab souk in Jerusalem, where every store sells something different, from food to clothing, and where the intoxicating fragrance of the incredible spices envelops us. We see amazing Roman ruins, including those at Beit She'an, Capernaum and Caesarea, and medieval Acre on the Mediterranean. Camels appear on the horizon as we drive through the Negev desert towards Masada, where we take the cable car up to the top of the mountain. History oozes from every corner here; on our way down the mountain we see the Dead Sea in the distance, and later we get to float in its buoyant waters and cover our bodies with Dead Sea mud. We take a relaxing boat ride on the Sea of Galilee, during which we sing and dance to Israeli songs with our new Egyptian friends and then visit the ancient town of Zvat (Safed) where artists sell their beautiful paintings.

Finally we spend two nights at a kibbutz at the northern end of Israel; at the end of each day we sit with our group sipping wine from local vineyards. Occasionally we hear the distant muffled thunder of gunfire across the border in Syria, a brief reminder of the realities of conflict so close to us. Viewing the stunning scenery at a lookout facing towards Syria, I find it difficult to comprehend that a civil war is raging there. Two men with weather-beaten faces are selling fruit on the side of the road near the vantage point, and one of them brings a basket of cherries for us all to share. Before we leave, my husband insists on paying them for the fruit. They accept the money under considerable protest and insist on making him a cup of Turkish coffee while the rest of the tour waits patiently on the bus.

Most importantly on this trip I fall in love with the inspiring joie de vivre of the Israeli people. I feel complete and I'm eager to get home where I will finally begin writing about my journey to find Benjamin.

Our flight home includes a connection in Moscow, and the experience is in sharp contrast to the previous three weeks we've just spent in Israel. After a red-eye flight we arrive at Domodedevo Airport around six thirty in the morning. Disorganized and testy employees are forced to work in a facility ill equipped to handle the number of planes and passengers that transit through it. We go in search of tea, coffee and breakfast, and it seems that anything goes here, including vodka snuck into the coffee shops in brown paper bags by Russian patrons who will add it to their morning juice.

We arrive back in Toronto tired but on an emotional high. It takes us a week to readjust to the time change and even longer to resettle into our daily routines, but I'm ready to begin writing now that I have made a full circle from where my search began.

§

I sometimes wonder if Benjamin is watching me as I piece together his short life and his struggle to survive. I have been unable to find anyone who may have known him in Skaryszew, Paris, Pithiviers or Auschwitz, and it seems unlikely that I ever will: born in 1905, Benjamin would be 107 years old, and it is doubtful that any of his contemporaries are still alive.

Yet I feel now as though I know him. I learned through my grandmother's stories that Benjamin, a lively boy, matured into a young man determined to live his life his way; a young man who chose seductive Paris over stolid England; a man who wooed and won over a beautiful young woman; a husband and father who loved his wife and children, and who did whatever he could to support them during peaceful times and to protect them in the face of adversity during the war; and a man who, in spite of his pacifist background, volunteered and fought for France.

Finally, because I now have that description of Benjamin's colouring, the black-and-white photograph that I look at each day comes alive. I see a proud, confident man, a man with luxuriant, wavy black hair and dark blue eyes — the same eyes I see in my young grandson.

And this is what I think now, when I look at that photograph: if Benjamin had survived, I would wrap my arms around him and hold him tight in hopes of taking away all the pain in his body and his soul.

EPILOGUE

Though unable to find any further information on Benjamin Albaum, I did receive printed materials and photographs from the archives in Radom, Poland, including Nazi ghetto records relating to several members of the Albaum family, and they are now registered at Yad Vashem. I also made contact with a group in France, the Association Mémoires du Convoi 6, in hopes of finding a survivor who may have remembered Benjamin. Two or possibly three people from Convoy 6 are alive at the time of this writing, but they are elderly and frail and I have decided not to put any of these people through further anguish in their twilight years by asking them to remember their own survival in the French and Nazi concentration camps. I provided a short biography of Benjamin along with his photograph to the association, and they included it in the revised edition of *Un train parmi tant d'autres*, a book created by the organization with individual biographies about some of the victims of Convoy 6.

Successful genealogy research can be extremely cathartic, especially with maternal and paternal families that are as large and intertwined as mine, lacking a clear distinction between the two sides. A vast, confusing mass of names and relationships starts to come into focus; the names become real people. I never knew Benjamin, yet as I uncovered increasingly more information, I acquired a greater understanding of him. Benjamin courageously left the Hasidic world in Poland at a very early age and embarked on a less orthodox life in France. Yet he was also a traditional man, and marriage and family were important to him. He worked hard to support Pessa and the children, and when faced with adversity he did his best to protect them by listing his children as French-born and by not providing Pessa's name to his interrogators. Despite his short stature, he must have possessed physical strength and resiliency: he survived fourteen months in Pithiviers, where he worked as a farm hand, and another ten months as a slave labourer in Auschwitz before his death. And it must have taken not only physical strength but also courage to hang on to life as long as he did. When I look at his photograph, I see a loving man, proud and tenacious, and this is the way I will remember him.

My search for Benjamin has changed me in profound ways, and I'm more aware of how fragile life is. And while I'm not a survivor, I have been indirectly affected by the murder of my family in France and Poland. Acutely aware of how much smaller our family became during the Holocaust, I frequently yearn for the dynamics of missed relationships. I often think about unwritten letters never exchanged and celebrations never shared. Every one of the six million Jews murdered in the Holocaust deserves a place in our memory and in our hearts. Benjamin Albaum is one of them and he will stay in my heart forever.

GLOSSARY

années folles: literally "the crazy years," refers to the 1920s.

brocanteur: a dealer of second-hand goods.

chuppah: a canopy, consisting of a cloth supported over four poles, under which a Jewish couple stands during the wedding ceremony; it represents a home that is open to everyone.

Hachomer Hatzaïr: the "Youth Guard"; a Socialist–Zionist youth movement founded in 1913 in Galicia, Austria-Hungary.

joie de vivre: literally "the joy of living."

ketubah: Jewish marriage contract.

Kotel: comes from the Hebrew HaKotel HaMa'aravi meaning Western Wall; one of the most sacred places for Jews, it is the last remaining standing section of the temple mount in the Old City of Jerusalem and dates from the second temple, making it more than 2,000 years old.

mazel tov: congratulations or best wishes.

mikvah: a ritual bath about the size of a small swimming pool and built to strict specifications; dating back to biblical times, they are used separately by Jewish men and women; immersion in a mikvah is required after occurrences that may be considered impure.

Old City: originally built by King David in 1004 BCE, it is a walled city in the center of Jerusalem and home to several ethnic and religious groups.

pogrom: a Russian word referring to violent attacks aimed at Jews during the 19th and 20th centuries.

sheitel: a wig worn by Orthodox women after they are married.

Shoah: biblical name meaning "calamity"; frequently used in Europe in reference to the Holocaust.

shtetl: a small Jewish village.

traifener medina: a Yiddish phrase referring to the unkosher world; some orthodox Jews feared the influence of the non-Jewish world as a place filled with non-kosher foods and behaviours forbidden by Jewish law.

tzedakah: a religious obligation of giving to those less fortunate.

Vel d'Hiv: shortened name of the Rafle du Vélodrome d'Hiver, a sports stadium in Paris where most of the Jewish victims of the July 17, 1942, round up were temporarily confined.

Yad Vashem: the official memorial to the Jewish victims of the Holocaust and to those gentiles who saved Jewish lives during World War II; located in Israel near Jerusalem, it comprises several museums along with research and educational centers; it also holds the database of Shoah Victims' names.

ACKNOWLEDGEMENTS

Thank you seems hardly enough for Marie-Lynn Hammond, my editor. Marie-Lynn patiently guided me, asked the right questions and understood my passion in telling this story. To Greg Ioannou, Publisher, Meghan Behse, Assistant Publisher, Kate Unrau, Copy Editor, along with Emily Niedoba and the entire staff at Iguana Books, my sincere thanks. To Jane Warren, who steered me in the right direction in finding the perfect editor, and Marilyn Biderman who made valuable suggestions, thank you both.

My husband has been unwavering in his support, enduring my absences while I wrote in solitude late into the night. Bob's love and encouragement never falters; he is my biggest fan, and I am so grateful to share my life with him.

To my children, who have been with me every step of the way and who patiently followed the story as it unfolded, thank you. To the rest of my family, including my grandchildren, brother, nieces and cousins, along with the entire Kroll family and my friends, thank you all for your support.

Dearest Celine, who welcomed me into her family in Paris and opened her soul to speak about her past, I am honoured to call you cousin.

My thanks to Ruth Frankel, whose creative writing class, along with her encouragement, enabled me not only to complete this book but also to submit my short story for publication.

My only disappointment is that my parents Carole and Bernard did not live long enough to see this memoir published. Their unconditional love and support propelled me to research and write this memoir.

Iguana Books
iguanabooks.com

If you enjoyed *A Stone for Benjamin*...
Look for other books coming soon from Iguana Books! Subscribe to our blog for updates as they happen.

iguanabooks.com/blog/

You can also learn more about Fiona Gold Kroll and her upcoming work on her website and blog.

fionagoldkroll.com

If you're a writer ...
Iguana Books is always looking for great new writers, in every genre. We produce primarily ebooks but, as you can see, we do the occasional print book as well. Visit us at iguanabooks.com to see what Iguana Books has to offer both emerging and established authors.

iguanabooks.com/publishing-with-iguana/

If you're looking for another good book ...
All Iguana Books books are available on our website. We pride ourselves on making sure that every Iguana book is a great read.

iguanabooks.com/bookstore/

Visit our bookstore today and support your favourite author.